JEB
STUART

Other titles in *Historical American Biographies*

Annie Oakley
Legendary Sharpshooter
ISBN 0-7660-1012-0

John Wesley Powell
Explorer of the Grand Canyon
ISBN 0-89490-783-2

Benjamin Franklin
Founding Father and Inventor
ISBN 0-89490-784-0

Lewis and Clark
Explorers of the Northwest
ISBN 0-7660-1016-3

Buffalo Bill Cody
Western Legend
ISBN 0-7660-1015-5

Martha Washington
First Lady
ISBN 0-7660-1017-1

Clara Barton
Civil War Nurse
ISBN 0-89490-778-6

Paul Revere
Rider for the Revolution
ISBN 0-89490-779-4

Jeb Stuart
Confederate Cavalry General
ISBN 0-7660-1013-9

Robert E. Lee
Southern Hero of the Civil War
ISBN 0-89490-782-4

Jefferson Davis
President of the Confederacy
ISBN 0-7660-1064-3

Stonewall Jackson
Confederate General
ISBN 0-89490-781-6

Jesse James
Legendary Outlaw
ISBN 0-7660-1055-4

Susan B. Anthony
Voice for Women's Voting Rights
ISBN 0-89490-780-8

Thomas Alva Edison
Inventor
ISBN 0-7660-1014-7

Historical American Biographies

JEB STUART
Confederate Cavalry General

Lynda Pflueger

Enslow Publishers, Inc.

44 Fadem Road	PO Box 38
Box 699	Aldershot
Springfield, NJ 07081	Hants GU12 6BP
USA	UK

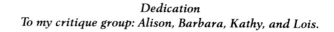

Dedication
To my critique group: Alison, Barbara, Kathy, and Lois.

Library of Congress Cataloging-in-Publication Data

Pflueger, Lynda.
    Jeb Stuart: Confederate cavalry general / Lynda Pflueger.
       p.   cm. — (Historical American biographies)
    Includes bibliographical references (p.) and index.
    Summary: Traces the life of the famous Confederate general from his
childhood in Virginia through his West Point education and brilliant
military career to his death following the Battle of Yellow Tavern.
    ISBN 0-7660-1013-9
    1. Stuart, Jeb, 1833–1864—Juvenile literature. 2. Generals—
Confederate States of America—Biography—Juvenile literature.
3. Confederate States of America. Army—Biography—Juvenile
literature. 4. United States—History—Civil War, 1861–1865—Cavalry
operations—Juvenile literature. [1. Stuart, Jeb, 1833–1864.
2. Generals. 3. United States—History—Civil War, 1861–1865.]
I. Title. II. Series.
E467.1.S9P48 1998
973.7'42—dc21
                                    97-4367
                                       CIP
                                       AC

Printed in the United States of America

10 9 8 7 6 5 4 3 2 1

Illustration Credits: Enslow Publishers, Inc., pp. 14, 101; Kansas State
Historical Society, Topeka, Kansas, p. 34; Library of Congress, pp. 6, 42,
46, 114; Massachusetts Commandery Military Order of the Loyal
Legion and the U.S. Army Military History Institute, pp. 12, 50, 55, 61,
86, 110; Virginia Historical Society, Richmond, Virginia, p. 24; Special
Collections Division of the United States Military Academy Library,
West Point, New York, p. 22; The Museum of the Confederacy,
Richmond, Virginia, photography by Katherine Wetzel, p. 75; National
Archives, p. 63, 102.

Cover Illustration: Corel (Background); Library of Congress (Inset).

CONTENTS

James Ewell Brown (Jeb) Stuart liked to wear a gray coat lined in red silk, golden spurs, an ostrich feather in his hat, and white buckskin gloves. Despite his showy appearance, he took his command seriously.

1

SCOUT AND RAIDER

In the spring of 1862, the Union Army under command of General George B. McClellan was preparing to strike the Confederate capital of Richmond. McClellan's goal was to end the Civil War with one major battle. Instead of taking his army over land, he chose to float his forces down the Potomac River to Fort Monroe. The fort was located between the York and James rivers on the tip of the Virginia Peninsula. From there, he would march his army up the peninsula to Richmond. "I will bring you face to face with the rebels," McClellan promised his men.[1]

Moving an Army

It took three weeks to move McClellan's army, and 400 ships to transport 121,500 men, 14,952 horses and mules, 1,150 wagons, 44 artillery batteries, 74 ambulances, pontoon bridges, provisions for all the men and livestock, tents, and telegraph wire.[2]

Slowly and cautiously, McClellan worked his way up the peninsula until he was only five miles from Richmond. His army was spread out for over twenty miles along the Chickahominy River. He brought up his big guns, 101 pieces of artillery, and planned to blast his way into the town.

Outnumbered and outgunned, General Robert E. Lee, commander of the Confederate forces, devised a bold plan to save the capital. He hoped to pull McClellan's attention away from Richmond by attacking his army's most vulnerable point.

Stuart's Orders

Suspecting that the right flank of McClellan's army was unprotected, Lee sent his cavalry commander, Colonel James Ewell Brown Stuart, on a scouting expedition. Lee ordered Stuart to explore the territory occupied by McClellan's right flank and report back its location and numbers. Stuart was also ordered to disrupt the Union Army's supply and communication lines.

After receiving his orders, Stuart selected twelve hundred horsemen to accompany him on his raid. At two o'clock in the morning on June 12, he awakened them by announcing, "Gentlemen, in ten minutes every man must be in his saddle!"[3] He told no one his destination. Many of the men thought they were going to the Shenandoah Valley to join Stonewall Jackson's army.

It turned into a sweltering, muggy day as they rode steadily northward. At Turner's Tavern they veered left and crossed over the Richmond, Fredericksburg, and Potomac railroad tracks. By nightfall they had traveled twenty-two miles and camped a few miles north of Ashland, Virginia. They lit no campfires so their location would not be apparent.

At first light on June 13, flares were sent up to signal the beginning of the day's march. They were too close to the enemy for bugles to be sounded. As they traveled in an easterly direction, it soon became apparent that they were not headed for the Shenandoah Valley. At this point Stuart informed several of his key commanders of his orders.

Hanover Court House

Stuart sent scouts out ahead of the main body of men. Later that morning, the scouts reported sighting

Union cavalry, about one hundred fifty men, up ahead at Hanover Court House. Stuart dispatched Fitzhugh Lee and his men to go around the town and block the Union cavalry's retreat. He did not want them to sound an alarm. Then he marched forward to confront them. The Northern horsemen chose to flee instead of fight. Due to the swampy terrain, Lee's men were unable to intercept them.

Stuart continued to move forward cautiously. He knew that an attack by Union troops, at this point, would delay his march and jeopardize his mission. Carefully he approached a bridge over Totopotomoy Creek. Union horsemen were nearby, but they simply watched the Confederates as they crossed. A mile from the bridge, however, the Union troops decided to take a stand. One hundred Union horsemen stood on the crest of a hill, ready for battle.

"Form fours! Draw sabers! Charge!" Stuart ordered.[4] Four abreast they attacked, yelling and waving their sabers. Their sudden assault overcame the Union troopers, who scattered in confusion. The Union cavalry fell back toward their camp in the village of Old Church. A mile before they reached the village, the Union troops received reinforcements and again formed a battle line. Stuart's men charged and broke through it. Finally, the battle reached the Union camp and the Confederate horsemen destroyed it.

Courthouses

Williamsburg and Yorktown were the main towns on the Virginia Peninsula. Because of the long distance between them, courthouses were built at Hanover, Charles City, and New Kent. The courthouses served as gathering places for local citizens and became focal points on the country roads of the region.

At this point Stuart had to decide whether to go back the way he had come or ride completely around McClellan's army. He had obtained the information he needed. The right flank of the Union Army was unprotected and vulnerable to attack, but he feared that if he returned the same way he had come, he would call attention to that fact. Keeping his uncertainty to himself, he decided to continue his circuit around the Union Army.

He ordered his column to move forward. Realizing they were in great danger, one of his men commented, "I think . . . the quicker we move now the better."[5] Stuart agreed and ordered the column to move forward at a trot.

Turnstall Station

Later that day, near Turnstall Station, one of Stuart's scouts, John Mosby, was riding ahead of the main

McClellan's army is shown here camped on the Virginia Peninsula, where Stuart's cavalry managed to carry out its successful raid.

column and came across Union cavalry. He was alone and his horse was too tired to make a run for it. Since the Union troopers were not close enough to get a good look at him, Mosby decided to take a chance and resorted to a bluff. He drew his saber, turned his horse around, and waved to the Union horsemen to join him. He hoped they would think he was one of them. They sat in their saddles and watched Mosby for several seconds. Then Stuart's column came into view and they fled.

When the Southern horsemen reached Turnstall Station, they overwhelmed the Union infantry stationed there. Then they harassed a passing train, burned a railroad bridge, and plundered and burned a wagon train.

Although his men were weary, Stuart pushed them on toward the town of Talleysville, five and a half miles away. When they reached the town they found well-stocked Union sutler's stores. Sutlers were peddlers who sold items, often at inflated prices, that the United States government did not provide to soldiers. The hungry Confederate soldiers feasted on figs, beef, tongue, pickles, candy, ketchup, preserves, lemons, cakes, sausages, molasses, crackers, and canned meats.[6]

At 10:00 P.M., Stuart let his men stop to feed their horses and rest for an hour. Then they rode through the night. At 5:00 A.M. on the morning of June 14, they reached the Chickahominy River and found it uncrossable. The banks of the river were swollen due to heavy rains upstream. Stuart's men cut down trees at the river's edge, attempting to make a temporary bridge, but the trees were not long enough and fell into the river.

Stuart knew that the Union Army was on his trail and it would only be a matter of time before it reached him. He sat in his saddle and stroked his beard as he thought. His scouts reported the ruins

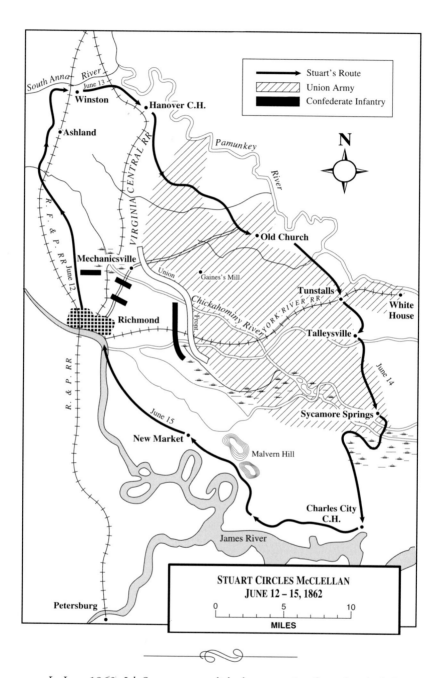

STUART CIRCLES McCLELLAN
JUNE 12 – 15, 1862

→	Stuart's Route	
▨	Union Army	
▮	Confederate Infantry	

South Anna River
June 13
Winston
Hanover C.H.
Ashland
Pamunkey
River
N
R. F. & P. RR
June 12
VIRGINIA CENTRAL RR
Old Church
Mechanicsville
Union
Gaines's Mill
Tunstalls
White House
Richmond
Chickahominy River
YORK RIVER RR
Talleysville
Front
R. & P. RR
June 14
Sycamore Springs
June 15
New Market
Malvern Hill
Charles City C.H.
James River
Petersburg

0   5   10
MILES

In June 1862, Jeb Stuart accomplished an amazing feat when he led his cavalry completely around Union General McClellan's army in only three days. This map shows the route Stuart took on his mission.

of an old bridge a mile away. He examined the bridge and decided to repair it. Two of his men, who had experience building bridges, came forward to rebuild it. An abandoned warehouse provided the necessary wood. The bridge was completed in three hours. By one o'clock that afternoon, the entire column had crossed the river. As the last horsemen set the bridge on fire, a small group of Union cavalry appeared on the other side of the river.

The Confederate troops traveled another seven miles to Charles City Court House before Stuart let his men rest. At dusk he set out with two of his couriers for Richmond, twenty-eight miles away. He left orders for the main column to resume its march at eleven o'clock that evening. During the night Stuart stopped only once for coffee and a few minutes rest. On Sunday morning, June 15, he rode into Richmond and made his report to General Robert E. Lee.

Stuart had achieved an amazing feat. He had ridden nearly one hundred fifty miles in three days, obtained the information he needed, and destroyed or confiscated a considerable amount of Union property. Stuart's raid thoroughly embarrassed the Northern army while raising Southern morale in the process. Overnight, he became a celebrity and hero known as Jeb Stuart, for his first name was replaced by his initials.

2

YOUNG STUART

James Ewell Brown Stuart was the seventh child and youngest son of Archibald Stuart, born December 2, 1795, and Elizabeth Letcher Pannill, born on June 4, 1801. His father was charming, witty, and enjoyed a good time, but his mother had "no special patience with nonsense."[1] Archibald and Elizabeth were married on June 16, 1817, and raised their family on a farm called Laurel Hill in Patrick County, Virginia. Elizabeth had inherited the farm from her grandfather, William Letcher.

Archibald Stuart was a lawyer and elected public official. Because of his profession, he was often away from home. He served one term in the United

William Letcher
William Letcher was a folk hero in Patrick County. He supported the independence of the American colonies and was shot and killed in June 1780 in his home by a British sympathizer. His family erected a monument in his honor on the grounds of Laurel Hill.

States House of Representatives, was a delegate to the Virginia Constitutional Convention, and was elected to the Virginia Senate. In her husband's absence, Elizabeth Stuart managed the family farm. They owned a small number of slaves who worked the land. At that time, the farmers in Patrick County grew tobacco and corn, and raised livestock.

James was born at eleven-thirty on the morning of February 6, 1833, on his family's farm. He grew up in a rural, isolated community where he played with his four brothers and six sisters, did his share of farm chores, and roamed the hills surrounding his home.

During his childhood he developed a love of animals, particularly horses. Stuart often referred to horses "with much the same feeling and familiarity" as he did his "family and friends."[2] He spent a great deal of his youth in the saddle.

His older brother, William Alexander, liked to tell a story about James's encounter with a hornet's

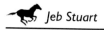

nest that occurred when James was nine years old and William fifteen. The boys came across a huge nest hanging from a tree and decided to destroy it. They climbed the tree, intending to knock the nest to the ground with sticks. As they approached, the hornets flew out of their nest and stung the boys. William jumped out of the tree and ran. James, however, stuck to it despite the pain of numerous stings and managed to dislodge the nest. Afterward, William Alexander concluded that his little brother would make a good soldier.

Schooling

In order to continue his education, James left home when he was twelve. He spent three years attending boarding school in Wytheville, Virginia. Before he left, his mother asked him to kneel before her and take an oath never to drink a drop of liquor. He kept his word until the day he died.

A short time after leaving home, he became homesick and wrote begging for letters from his family. "Have mercy upon a poor, little, insignificant whelp away from his mammy," he wrote.[3] In another letter to an older cousin, he proudly reported that he had had the good fortune "not to have a single fight since I have been going to school."[4] Then he added that this achievement was "not from cowardice either."[5]

In 1848, at the age of fifteen, James enrolled in Emory & Henry College. It was the first institution of higher learning founded in southwestern Virginia. Attending the school for two years, he studied mechanics and classical literature, and joined a literary and debating society. One day while giving a speech, he became so absorbed in what he was saying, he forgot where he was and fell off the stage. Also while attending Emory & Henry, he joined the Methodist Church during a revival in 1849.

Since he did not come from a wealthy family and would not inherit property, James knew he would have to choose from one of what he called the "hireling professions."[6] He would have to hire himself out to work in either the legal, medical, engineering, or military profession.

West Point

While attending Emory & Henry College, James became interested in going to the United States Military Academy at West Point. At the time, West Point provided the best education the country could offer a young man. An appointment to the academy had to be obtained through a congressional representative. This was probably a matter he discussed with his father when he ran for a seat in Congress in 1848. Although his father lost the election, the first official act of his successful

opponent, Thomas Hamlet Averett, was to appoint James to West Point.

James left Wytheville for West Point in late June 1850. On the way, he stopped in Washington, D.C., to tour the city. In a letter he wrote to a relative, he mentioned seeing President Zachary Taylor twice while walking around the city streets. He described Taylor as "a plain looking old fellow with a slight squat as he walks."[7] He spent part of a day visiting the United States Senate and commented that he thought Daniel Webster was "the finest looking man in the Senate" but added, "of all the pleasant speakers give me Jeff Davis of Mississippi."[8] Later in the day, he visited the House of Representatives, finding it to be "a rowdy place compared to the Senate."[9]

The next day he took a train to Baltimore, Maryland, and then a steamboat to New York. After a brief stay in New York City, he took a night cruise up the Hudson River to West Point.

During the summer months, West Point cadets moved out of their barracks and into a tent city in the nearby woods. Shortly after arriving, James was assigned to a tent pitched over a wooden platform and exchanged his civilian clothes for a cadet's uniform. The uniform consisted of high-top black shoes, white trousers, a short gray coat with a stiff collar and three rows of brass buttons, and a black leather cap with a pompon.[10]

First-year students at West Point were called plebes. They lived under the constant scrutiny and supervision of upperclassmen who often harassed them. During the summer, plebes were drilled by their cadet officers three times a day in infantry tactics and once a day on the use of artillery. Somehow, while living outside in the woods, James managed to learn the military routine and how to keep his white pants clean.[11]

Within a month, Stuart had adjusted to military life and wrote to a cousin, saying, "So far as I know of no profession more desirable than that of the soldier."[12] He particularly enjoyed the social life at camp and was impressed by the ceremonies, parades, and prominent visitors.

On the first day of September, the tents were taken down and the cadets marched into barracks to begin their first year of classes. James shared a sparsely furnished room with Judson D. Bigham from Indiana and Charles G. Rogers from Virginia. He considered himself lucky to be with two "very studious and clever fellows."[13]

James's classmates called him a "Bible class man" because he attended Bible classes regularly. They also gave him the nickname "Beauty." This was not because they thought he was good-looking, but exactly the opposite. He had a small chin and his face was often bruised due to numerous fistfights.

This photograph shows the United States Military Academy at West Point as it looked in the 1850s.

Most of his fights were with larger students and he was often beaten, but he always came back for more.[14] With his never-give-up attitude, he gained the respect of his fellow cadets.

During his first year at West Point, James took classes in English, mathematics, and French. He fared better than he expected. At the end of the year, out of a class of seventy-one, he placed eighth in mathematics, fifteenth in French, and twelfth in English.

James began his second year at West Point with rank. He was appointed corporal of the corps, which was the third highest rank available for a cadet in his second year. Once again he studied mathematics and French. Also part of the curriculum were drawing classes and riding exercises. He established himself as "one of the best horsemen in his class."[15] He enjoyed the riding drills and found the "Yankee" cadets to be amusing. He felt they were "ridiculous figures" on "horseback."[16] Northern cadets were not used to riding horses, but the cadets from the rural South grew up on horseback.

Many times in his letters to family and friends, James mentioned the tensions that were building between the North and the South over the issue of slavery. He felt that Northerners did not understand that slavery had become a necessity in the South. In the industrialized North, slavery had become less

The picture, probably taken shortly after their graduation from West Point in 1854, shows James Ewell Brown Stuart (center) and two of his friends, Stephen Dill Lee (right) and George Washington Custis Lee (left).

common. Because the South was agricultural, farmers depended on slaves to work the land.

In September 1852, Colonel Robert E. Lee was appointed superintendent of West Point. Over the next two years, James became a favorite of the Lee family and visited their home often. He was attracted to Mary Custis Lee, the superintendent's daughter, and developed a special friendship with his wife, Mary Lee.

While attending West Point, James became interested in several young women. He preferred ladies from Virginia because the more he saw of Northern girls, the more he was "convinced of their inferiority in every respect to our Virginia ladies, in beauty especially."[17]

During his fourth and final year at West Point, James was given the title of cavalry officer due to his superior horsemanship. He spent many hours that winter practicing—swinging his saber at dummy heads that sat on top of posts in the academy riding hall. He also excelled in classes on infantry, artillery, and cavalry tactics. Because of his lack of drawing skills, he placed poorly in his civil engineering class even though he found the course to be the most interesting one he ever pursued. He graduated in July 1854, and ranked thirteenth in a class of forty-six. Originally the class had been composed of 102 members.

3

THE FRONTIER

S tuart spent part of the summer of 1854 visiting
family and friends in Virginia. He enjoyed the
free time, but was impatient to get on with his
Army career. Finally his orders arrived and he
received a commission as a second lieutenant in the
Mounted Rifles. He was ordered to report to Fort
Clark in western Texas by October 15.

After outfitting himself in New York for his trip,
he briefly visited a cousin at West Point and set out
for Texas. He had to pass through New Orleans, but
due to a yellow fever epidemic there, he was unable
to enter the city. This prompted the War Department
to extend his leave. He waited in St. Louis, Missouri,

until November 29 when he booked passage on a steamer out of New Orleans.

When the steamer left the mouth of the Mississippi River and entered the Gulf of Mexico, a storm hit. The rocking and rolling of the boat made Stuart seasick. He was so sick that it took twelve hours after the boat reached Galveston, Texas, for him to finally realize they were tied up to dry land.

From Galveston, Stuart continued his boat journey to Indianola, a Texas port located between Galveston and Corpus Christi. From Indianola he took a mail boat to Corpus Christi, where he stayed until December 29. Then he joined a wagon train headed for Laredo, four hundred fifty miles away.

He described the country he traveled through as "entirely uninhabited prairie . . . clothed in cactus."[1] One day, he found a beautiful flower blooming along the roadside. Since he loved flowers, he almost picked it. Instead he decided to leave it as "an ornament to the solitude."[2]

In Laredo, Stuart learned that his company was on an expedition, hunting renegade Mescalero Apache and Comanche Indians. His unit was on its way to Fort Davis, located in the heart of western Texas between the Pecos River and the Rio Grande. When Stuart arrived at Fort Davis on January 29, he discovered that his company was fifty miles farther west. He rested briefly and set out to join them.

Finally, two months after leaving St. Louis, he joined his unit. Commanded by Major John S. Simonson, the expedition scoured West Texas for months. In March 1855, Stuart wrote to his cousin, "We have threaded every trail, clambered every precipice and penetrated every ravine for hundreds of miles around" and "we have not been able to find Mr. Comanche."[3]

He added that many times the terrain was so rough he had to dismount and lead his horse through it. "I wore out a pair of very thick shoes . . . and would have been barefooted but for a pair of embroidered slippers," he wrote.[4] The slippers were given to him by a girlfriend while he was at West Point. He commented that she probably had no idea they would eventually walk "Comanches trails."[5]

Despite the hardships, Stuart enjoyed the scenery. In another letter, he wrote that the Blue quail, also known as the Rio Grande quail, was "the prettiest bird I ever saw."[6] He thought the prairie dogs were one of the most remarkable animals in Texas and spent many hours observing them. He commented that the prairie wolves howled every night, but the "most mournful cry" was that of the mountain lion—a large, powerful wildcat also called a panther.[7] With a companion he set out to hunt "His Panthership" but was unsuccessful.[8]

During the expedition, Stuart took command of the unit's only piece of artillery. At one point, it became difficult to transport the gun through a narrow mountain pass. It appeared the gun might have to be left behind. Stuart, not willing to part with the equipment unless his commander ordered it, had the gun lowered down the mountainside with ropes. Amazed, his commander told him "that he had never expected to see me bring the artillery down that mountain."[9]

The next day they discovered an abandoned American Indian village, and the following morning they met up with an infantry unit from El Paso, Texas. The foot soldiers were also hunting Indians. That evening both companies set up camp "in a deep and narrow valley or *arroyo*, clothed in luxuriant grass."[10] The men put their horses out to graze and lit their campfires. Suddenly a gust of wind swept through the valley and spread the campfires all "over the grass like a tornado, setting the whole prairie in a blaze in a few moments."[11] The fire swept through the entire camp, burning bridles, saddles, blankets, caps, coats, and anything else in its way. Many of the horses were singed.

Stuart stayed in West Texas for three more months. During that time he grew a reddish-brown beard and mustache. In a letter to a friend back east, Stuart wrote that his beard had greatly changed his

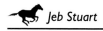

appearance and that his friend would not recognize him. Stuart wore a beard for the rest of his life.

During the spring of 1855, Secretary of War Jefferson Davis established two new cavalry regiments, the 1st and 2nd Cavalry. The troublesome American Indian situation on the frontier concerned him. He felt that the Mounted Rifles, infantry men on horseback, were outdated. He saw the need for a "big, swift-striking force able to find the enemy in his own country and endure long campaigns."[12] Davis chose the most capable and distinguished officers he could find to lead the new regiments.

Stuart was delighted when he received an appointment as a second lieutenant in the 1st Cavalry regiment. Prior to this time, his commission as a second lieutenant had been a brevet (temporary) rank. His new appointment was permanent. He was ordered to report to Fort Leavenworth, in the Kansas Territory. Stuart arrived at Fort Leavenworth in July 1855 and was appointed quartermaster for his new regiment.

Flora Cooke

During the summer of 1855, Stuart became attracted to a petite young woman by the name of Flora Cooke. Her father, Lieutenant Colonel Philip St. George Cooke, commanded the Second Regiment of Dragoons—heavily armed and mounted soldiers.

Twenty-year-old Flora had just completed finishing school. A finishing school is a private girls' school that stresses training in cultural subjects and social activities. Although her parents wanted her to make her social debut in Philadelphia society, she insisted on visiting them at Fort Leavenworth.

The first time Stuart saw Flora, she was riding a large and nervous horse while officers were reviewing troops. She handled the skittish animal like an expert. Later Stuart asked her to go riding with him. Before long, they were riding together almost every evening. In less than two months, they were engaged to be married. Stuart summarized his rapid courtship with a variation of a famous Latin quote, saying, "I came; I saw; I was conquered."[13]

The couple planned an elaborate church wedding in November at Fort Riley, Kansas, where Colonel Cooke had been transferred. However, two months before the scheduled wedding day, their romance was interrupted when Stuart's regiment went on a raid. When he returned, Stuart received word that his father had died.

Due to these circumstances, the couple chose to be married in a simple ceremony on November 14. The wedding was a small family affair. Flora wore her white graduation dress. Her glowing blue eyes and beautiful complexion dazzled her bridegroom.[14] The couple stayed at Fort Riley for a short time.

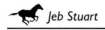

Then they returned to Fort Leavenworth and set up housekeeping in what Stuart jokingly called his "ranch." The ranch consisted of two rooms and a kitchen.[15]

On December 20, 1855, Stuart was promoted to first lieutenant, after being in the 1st Cavalry for only five months. This type of rapid promotion was rare in peacetime. Taken by surprise, his father-in-law, Colonel Cooke, wrote to his nephew, John Esten Cooke, "Flora was married, rather suddenly—to Mr. Stuart of Virginia . . . He is a remarkably fine, promising, pure young man, and has had so far an extraordinary promotion. He is First Lieutenant, 1st Cavalry."[16]

Bleeding Kansas

The following year Stuart was away from home a great deal. His command tried to keep the situation with the Cheyenne under control and maintain peace among the settlers. The issue of whether Kansas should be a free or slave state was ripping apart the state. Proslavery bands from Missouri were invading Kansas and attacking antislavery settlers. This produced a small-scale civil war that was called "Bleeding Kansas."

On a peacekeeping mission in June 1856, Stuart met John Brown, an abolitionist who had led several violent raids in Kansas. Brown and his sons were accused of killing five supporters of slavery at

The Kansas-Nebraska Act
In 1854, Congress passed the Kansas-Nebraska Act, which specified that the citizens of Kansas and Nebraska would decide at the polls whether their territories would become free or slave states. The act also repealed the Missouri Compromise, which had prohibited slavery in the territories. This angered Northerners who opposed slavery and increased the tension between the North and the South.

Pottawatomie Creek on May 24. In retaliation, a proslavery faction from Missouri captured some of Brown's men, including one of his sons. Brown attacked the group. After a gun battle, the Missourians surrendered and were taken prisoner. Stuart was part of the detachment sent to order Brown to release his prisoners and disband.

Cheyenne Raids

While the Army was trying to keep peace among the settlers, Cheyenne renegades began raiding and killing settlers in western Kansas. The cavalry was ordered to undertake a campaign against the Cheyenne to punish them and reassert the government's authority by a show of force.

Six cavalry companies, three infantry companies, and a battery of artillery marched southeast in search of the Cheyenne. On July 29, they came upon three hundred Cheyenne warriors in battle formation. This was Stuart's first encounter with the Cheyenne in his eighteen months on the frontier. The confrontation occurred at Solomon's Fork in northwest Kansas. The troops charged, yelling wildly, with their swords drawn. When the two battle lines met, the Cheyenne broke their formation and fled. The troops chased after them.

While defending a comrade, Stuart was shot at from a distance of less than two feet. The bullet struck him in the chest, bounced off a bone, and

These members of the Kansas Free State Battery are standing near a cannon left over from the Mexican War. Groups like these engaged in bloody combat over the issue of slavery in the territories.

lodged in fatty tissue. Luckily, the bullet did not damage any of his vital organs.

The main part of the detachment continued to chase the Cheyenne. Stuart and five other wounded soldiers, accompanied by an infantry company, headed for Fort Kearny, one hundred twenty miles away. They had no compass and had to depend on friendly American Indian guides who had been left with them. On the sixth day of their journey, they awoke surrounded by a thick fog and found that their guides were gone. Stuart and his companions were lost, their food rations were running out, and some of the men had worn through their shoes and were walking barefoot.

As the situation grew worse, Stuart's leadership grew stronger. He volunteered to lead a scouting mission to search for Fort Kearny. Two other men joined him. They were ready to leave on the morning of August 15, but a dense fog held them back. They left at noon despite the fog and by late afternoon a storm hit. In an attempt to keep their saddles dry, they took them off their horses and sat on them. All they could do was bow their heads to the wind and rain. In the middle of the night they awoke to find that the grassy ravine where they had tied their horses had turned into a river. The water was rising rapidly. Quickly they moved their saddles and led their mounts to higher ground.

The following morning, wet, cold, and hungry, they continued their ride. The clouds concealed the sun and it was hard for them to determine in what direction they were traveling. At one point, the sun shone through the clouds and Stuart was able to determine that they were traveling in the wrong direction. He corrected their course, but they soon came upon a stream they could not cross.

He led the group upstream in hopes of finding a place to cross. Instead they found a trail and followed it until dark. During the night, the sky cleared. By observing the stars, Stuart determined that they were finally headed in the right direction.

The following morning they came upon a wagon road that had recently been used. Stuart realized the road connected Fort Leavenworth and Fort Kearny. Later that afternoon they arrived at Fort Kearny and a rescue party was sent to find the soldiers that had been left behind.

Stuart returned to Flora at Fort Leavenworth on August 17, 1856. In the first week of September, she gave birth to their first child, a girl. Stuart insisted that she be named Flora after her mother and proclaimed that he had "the prettiest and smartest baby in North America."[17] Over the next year and a half, the problem with the Cheyenne settled down and Stuart had time to enjoy his new family.

4

JOHN BROWN'S RAID

L ate in the evening on Sunday, October 16, 1859, a small band of men walked behind a horse-drawn wagon on a winding Maryland road, headed for Harpers Ferry, Virginia. Hidden under each man's winter clothing was a rifle. They called themselves the Provisional Army of the United States and their mission was to free their land of the "peculiar institution" of slavery "once and for all."[1] They were all dedicated to their cause and willing to die for it.

Their leader, John Brown, carefully chose Harpers Ferry as the place to begin their righteous

crusade. He needed the weapons housed there in the United States arsenal to arm the slaves he expected to rise up and join his rebellion. He planned to establish a base of operations in the mountains of Virginia from which he could easily raid Southern plantations and send slaves north to freedom.

After two hours of silent marching, the group crossed the Baltimore and Ohio Railroad bridge and headed for the armory buildings. They used a crowbar to break through the main gate and took the watchmen hostage. Once they held possession of the armory, they took over the rifle factory and other strategic positions in the town.

"The Secret Six"
Brown's activities were supported by a group of Northern abolitionists known as "The Secret Six." Members of the group included: Dr. Samuel Gridley Howe, a Boston educator and minister; Thomas Wentworth Higginson, a minister from Massachusetts; Theodore Parker, a minister from Boston; Franklin B. Sanborn, an editor and schoolmaster from Massachusetts; Gerrit Smith, a prominent landowner and former congressman from New York; and George L. Stearns, an industrialist and merchant from Massachusetts.

Early the next morning, the citizens of Harpers Ferry became aware of the assault. Volunteer militia from nearby towns in Maryland and Virginia came to their neighbors' assistance. Shots were fired and several of the raiders were killed or wounded. Finally, Brown and his men took refuge in the old engine house on the armory grounds.

The War Department

James Stuart was at the War Department in Washington, D.C., when rumors began to circulate that a slave rebellion was taking place in Harpers Ferry. He volunteered to take a message to Colonel Robert E. Lee in Arlington, Virginia. At the time, Lee was on leave from his post in Texas, trying to settle his father-in-law's estate. When Lee received the message, he left immediately for the War Department.

At the War Department, arrangements were made to send a detachment of ninety Marines to Harpers Ferry. Lee, accompanied by Stuart, went to talk with President James Buchanan at the White House. The president wanted "a strong show of military force."[2] He placed Lee in command of the operation. Stuart volunteered to accompany him as an aide. Lee gratefully accepted the services of his former West Point student.

Harpers Ferry

The Marine detachment was already on its way to
Harpers Ferry, so a special locomotive was sent to
transport Lee and Stuart. They joined the Marines a
mile outside of town around 10:00 P.M. Shortly after
arriving, Lee learned that the rumored three thousand raiders consisted of less than twenty men and
that they had taken a few of the town's prominent
citizens as hostages.

One of the hostages was Colonel Lewis W.
Washington, the great-grandnephew of George
Washington. Brown had seized two things that
Washington owned—a pistol that had been present-
ed to George Washington by the Marquis de
Lafayette and a sword that had been given to him by
King Frederick the Great of Prussia. Brown fancied
the idea of using George Washington's sword and
pistol in his crusade to free the slaves.

Lee ordered the Marines to march onto the
armory grounds and for everyone else to leave. After
he surveyed the situation, he asked the militia units
to return and surround the armory. Then he wrote
out a message to "the persons in the armory buildings."[3] He told them that if they surrendered
peacefully and turned over the weapons they had
stolen, he would protect them. He also warned them
that escape was impossible and if they chose to fight
he could not "answer for their safety."[4]

Lee offered the honor of storming the engine house to the Maryland militia. They declined, saying they had wives and children to think about and that the regular military was paid to do that kind of work. Lee also made the same offer to the Virginia militia. They declined for the same reasons. Finally, Lee offered the honor to Lieutenant Israel Green, the commander of the Marine detachment. Green thanked Lee for the honor and chose a party of twelve men from his company to storm the armory and another twelve men to stand in reserve. Lee instructed the Marines to use bayonets, not bullets, for fear they might injure the hostages.

By daylight all the arrangements for the assault on the engine house had been made. It was agreed that Stuart, under a white flag of truce, would deliver Lee's message. If he was unable to persuade the raiders to surrender, he would step away from the engine-house door and wave his hat as a signal to begin storming the building.

Stuart walked toward the engine-house door waving his white flag. He yelled that he had a message from Colonel Lee. The door opened about four inches and John Brown stood with his body placed against the door, pointing a cocked gun at Stuart. Stuart recognized him immediately. They had met three years before in Kansas. The two men discussed the terms for surrender. Finally, convinced

that no amount of discussion would resolve the situation, Stuart moved away from the door and waved his hat.

The Marines, led by Lieutenant Green, moved forward and began beating the engine-house door with sledgehammers. Green quickly realized that the sledgehammers were having no effect on the heavy door. He noticed a wooden ladder lying nearby and ordered his reserve force to pick it up and use it as a battering ram. They rammed the door twice and managed to break a small hole in the bottom.

Green crawled through the hole, followed by his men. He ran to the rear of the building and discovered Brown kneeling between two fire engines. When Brown cocked his gun, Green raised his sword and struck him several times on the neck and head. Brown fell to the floor, unconscious. Within three minutes, the Marines had taken over the engine house. Two Marines died in the assault along with

John Brown claimed that he had done no wrong. He believed he was morally right to lead his raid on Harpers Ferry.

two of Brown's men, but all thirteen of the hostages were safe.

When Brown was dragged outside, some of his captors thought he would die of his wounds. Stuart suspected he was faking unconsciousness and relieved him of his Bowie knife—a large single-edged hunting knife. Stuart kept the knife as a souvenir.

Later that morning, Lee sent Stuart and a group of Marines to Brown's farmhouse in Maryland, about four and a half miles away. There, they found a large supply of weapons, including over one thousand pikes—poles with metal points. They also found letters and documents pertaining to Brown's militant activities.

Governor Henry A. Wise of Virginia and other officials questioned Brown the following day. For three hours, he talked about his crusade and his disappointment that a large number of slaves had not revolted and joined him. Then Brown predicted the future concerning the question of slavery and the possibility of a civil war:

> You had better—all you people at the South—prepare yourselves for a settlement of that question that must come up for settlement sooner than you are prepared for it. The sooner you are prepared the better. You may dispose of me very easily; I am nearly disposed of now; but this question is still to be settled—this negro question I mean—the end of that is not yet.[5]

5

CIVIL WAR

John Brown was tried and found guilty of treason against the state of Virginia, conspiring to incite a slave rebellion, and murder. He was sentenced to hang on December 2, 1859. Many Northerners considered him a martyr because he was dying for his cause, but most Southerners thought he was a murdering madman. Fearful that Brown's supporters would try to rescue him, Virginia Governor Henry Wise allowed no civilians near the execution site. Fifteen hundred soldiers surrounded the open field where the scaffold was erected. The Virginia Military Institute sent its cadets, accompanied by

Major Thomas Jackson, to help maintain order in the town.

John Brown's raid added to the tensions that had been building between the North and the South over the issue of slavery. In the North, slavery had died a natural death because of industrialization and the availability of cheap labor provided by European immigrants. In the South, however, slavery flourished with the invention of the cotton gin. Developed by a Northern teacher, Eli Whitney, the machine separated the cotton fibers from cotton seed a hundred times faster than a person could by hand. This led to the expansion of the textile industry,

Uncle Tom's Cabin

In 1850, a Northern abolitionist named Harriet Beecher Stowe published a novel called Uncle Tom's Cabin. The book portrayed the cruelty of slavery as no other publication had before. More than three hundred thousand copies were sold in the United States in one year, and 1.5 million copies were printed worldwide. Southerners claimed the book was all lies. Northerners, who were unfamiliar with slavery, were shocked by the story. Many people, including Queen Victoria of England, wept after reading the book.[1]

UNCLE TOM'S CABIN;

OR,

LIFE AMONG THE LOWLY.

BY

HARRIET BEECHER STOWE.

VOL. I.

BOSTON:
JOHN P. JEWETT & COMPANY.
CLEVELAND, OHIO:
JEWETT, PROCTOR & WORTHINGTON.
1852.

This is the cover of Harriet Beecher Stowe's controversial book, Uncle Tom's Cabin.

and the demand for cotton soared until the Southern economy became dependent on slaves to produce it.

Growing cotton year after year depleted the soil in the South. Many Southerners looked longingly at new territories acquired by the United States as potential land to be developed. At the same time, the antislavery movement in the North grew stronger. Many Northerners believed that it was morally wrong for a person to own another person. Those who believed this were called abolitionists, and they wanted to put an end to slavery.

Stuart Returns to Kansas

Stuart's leave ended shortly after the incident at Harpers Ferry. On December 15, 1859, he returned to Kansas and the command of Company G, 1st Cavalry. His leave had been profitable. While in Washington, he had patented an invention called the sword hook, an attachment for cavalry sword belts. The device enabled a horseman to remove his sword and holder from his belt and attach it to his horse's saddle. This meant the horseman could dismount from his horse quickly without his sword getting in the way. The United States government paid Stuart five thousand dollars for the patent rights to the device. He would also receive a dollar for each sword hook the manufacturer sold.

During the spring of 1860, Stuart's company mounted a campaign against the Kiowa and Comanche. For three months he was away from his family and out of touch with what was going on nationally. Flora was expecting their second child in June.

In August, Stuart returned to Fort Riley and learned that Flora had given birth to "a fine son" on June 26, 1860.[2] He was named Philip St. George Cooke Stuart in honor of Flora's father. Stuart's reunion with his family was brief. After just a month, he left with four cavalry companies and two infantry divisions to establish Fort Wise on the Arkansas River, 387 miles away in the Arkansas wilderness.

The Election of 1860

The last straw in the conflict over slavery was the presidential election of 1860. Like most Southerners, Stuart was a Democrat. Shortly before the election of 1860, the Democratic party split three ways. Each section nominated its own presidential candidate. John C. Breckinridge of Kentucky became the Southern Democratic candidate. Stephen Douglas of Illinois was the Northern Democratic candidate. John Bell of Tennessee ran on the Constitutional Union ticket.

Because of the party split, no one Democratic candidate could win enough votes to be elected. The Republican candidate, Abraham Lincoln, won the election with 1,866,452 votes. Bell received 588,879 votes. Breckinridge got 849,781 votes, and Douglas got 1,376,975 votes. Lincoln did not carry any of the fifteen Southern states. In fact, in some of the Southern states his name did not even appear on the ballot.

News traveled slowly to the Arkansas frontier. A short time after the election of 1860, Stuart wrote to friends asking, "Who's President?"[3] Then on December 20, the same day that South Carolina withdrew from the Union, he commented in a letter to a friend, "I believe the north will yield what the south demands" and thereby prevent the breakup of the Union.[4]

Stuart was wrong. After South Carolina seceded, Mississippi, Florida, Alabama, Georgia, Louisiana, and Texas followed. On February 8, 1861, the Confederate States of America was formed.

Virginia Secedes

Stuart requested leave so he could join his family at Fort Riley. He wanted to see what his home state of Virginia would do. In a letter to his brother, William, he clearly stated his intentions. He would remain faithful to his home state, whatever its

This photograph of Abraham Lincoln was taken in 1858. When Lincoln was elected president of the United States in 1860, it caused some of the Southern states to secede from the Union.

decision. He wrote, "I go with Virginia."[5] Stuart was a loyal Southerner who believed in the institution of slavery.

His leave was delayed and Stuart did not reach Fort Riley until early April. He was there when Confederate forces fired on Fort Sumter in Charleston Harbor on April 14. The fort, a Union facility on South Carolina soil, was surrendered to the Confederates. After the fall of Fort Sumter, President Lincoln issued a proclamation calling for seventy-five thousand volunteers to serve ninety days to put down the rebellion. Virginia's quota was eight thousand men. Governor John Letcher of Virginia was furious. To Lincoln's demand he replied, "The people of this Commonwealth are freemen, not slaves."[6] He added that he would send no troops from Virginia. Two days later, Virginia seceded from the Union followed by Arkansas, Tennessee, and North Carolina. The Confederacy now consisted of eleven Southern, slaveholding states.

After receiving word that Virginia had seceded, Stuart packed up his family and left for St. Louis, Missouri. His mail was being held there and when he arrived, he found a letter from the War Department, informing him that he had been promoted to the rank of captain, effective April 22. After leaving St. Louis, Stuart took his family to

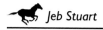

Cairo, Illinois, where he sent a letter of resignation to the adjutant general of the United States Army.

Then Stuart and his family took a steamboat to Memphis, Tennessee, and arrived in Wytheville, Virginia, on May 7. Stuart went on to Richmond by himself and stayed with his mother, Elizabeth. She had been living in the city for almost a year. One of his cousins, Peter W. Hairston, offered him a horse and volunteered to be his aide. On May 10 he was appointed a lieutenant colonel in the Provisional Army of Virginia. He was commissioned in the infantry because there were no cavalry posts available.

He wrote Flora, telling her he was leaving for the front at once and that he would be second in command to Colonel Thomas J. Jackson at Harpers Ferry. Stuart called Jackson an odd but committed soldier who had come from the Virginia Military Institute with his young cadets. He added that his mother had let him have Jo, one of the slaves from Laurel Hill, as a body servant for the duration of the war.

Stuart's Command

Jackson ignored Stuart's appointment in the infantry. Since Stuart had the cavalry experience and appropriate rank, Jackson consolidated all his cavalry companies under Stuart's command. He admired Stuart's creed—a statement of essential beliefs—which said: "If we oppose force to force we cannot win, for their resources are greater than ours. We must substitute *esprit* for numbers. Therefore I strive to inculcate in my men the spirit of the chase."[7]

Since Stuart was only twenty-nine years old at the time, many of the troopers resented his youth. Captain Turner Ashby, who also served in the cavalry on the frontier, refused to accept Stuart as his commander. Jackson resolved this problem by dividing the cavalry troops between the two men.

Before the end of May, Stuart wrote to Flora again. He was concerned about her father, Colonel Cooke. "He is wanted here very much," he wrote. "Why don't he come?"[8] Stuart wanted his father-in-law to see things the same way he had, and resign his commission in the United States Army so he could join the Confederacy.

6

STUART'S CAVALRY

Two weeks after Stuart arrived at Harpers Ferry, Brigadier General Joseph E. Johnston replaced Jackson as commander. Johnston was an old friend of Stuart's from the frontier. Shortly after his arrival, Stuart received a commission as a lieutenant colonel in the cavalry.

Johnston was convinced that Harpers Ferry was impossible to defend and withdrew his troops to Winchester, Virginia. The Union Army, commanded by General Robert Patterson, was only thirteen miles away in Martinsburg. In between Johnston's troops and the Union Army, Stuart established his headquarters at Bunker Hill.

While camped at Bunker Hill, Stuart set out to train his men. Often he would take them behind enemy lines. On one such occasion he ordered a small group of his troopers to dismount and confront the enemy on foot. When they were within two hundred yards of the Union soldiers, he ordered them to with'draw by marching backward and firing their guns at the same time. When they reached their horses, he would not let them ride away faster than at a trot.

As soon as they reached a safe distance from the advancing troops, Stuart gave his troopers a brief lecture. He told them they were "brave fellows and patriotic" but they had a great deal to learn.[1] First, he wanted them to understand that "a good man on a good horse can never be caught" and "cavalry can trot away from anything."[2]

Then he told them, "We gallop toward the enemy, and trot away, always."[3] Stuart was teaching his men to boldly gallop toward the enemy in

Stuart once told his wife that General Joseph E. Johnston, pictured here, was the best friend he had in the Confederate Army.

battle and to calmly trot away as if unaffected by the danger they had faced.

Suddenly they heard the sound of an artillery shell as it flew through the air above their heads. "I've been waiting for that," Stuart told them.[4] Since his men had never been in battle before, he wanted them to know what an artillery shell sounded like. Earlier in the day he had observed the Northern artillery and he knew they would "shoot too high."[5]

After spending a few days in training with Stuart, his men gained the confidence they needed to do the job he demanded of them. Every road and path in a fifty-mile range between the Confederate and Union armies had to be monitored twenty-four hours a day. Stuart often accompanied his men on

Description of Jeb Stuart
William W. Blackford, an engineer from Abingdon, Virginia, described Stuart at the time as: "A little above medium height, broad shouldered and powerfully built, ruddy complexion and blue-gray eyes which could flash fire on the battlefield, or sparkle with the merry glance which ladies love. Stuart was then about 29 years of age."[6] Blackford eventually became Stuart's aide.

picket duty. He demanded no more of his troopers than he did of himself.

Falling Waters

Due to his men's diligence, Stuart was able to inform Johnston when the Northern army marched out of Martinsburg and headed toward Winchester on July 1, 1861. Johnston sent Jackson's brigade and Stuart's horsemen to engage the advancing troops. Their orders were to observe the Union Army's movements but to fall back if outnumbered.

Stuart's cavalry met Jackson's troops near a church called Falling Waters, about five miles south of the Potomac River. While Stuart guarded his flank, Jackson confronted the Union troops in order to determine their strength. He soon realized he was outnumbered and began to withdraw slowly while continuing to fight. As the infantry withdrew, Stuart's men clashed with the Northern cavalry. Their fighting spread out over the countryside.

At one point, Stuart became separated from his men and came across a group of Union soldiers. They were standing on the other side of a rail fence. Stuart rode up to the fence and ordered them to take it down. Because of his blue coat and old United States Army trousers, they thought he was one of their officers and quickly complied with his request. When they were finished, Stuart ordered

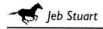

them to throw down their weapons and surrender. The Union soldiers thought the woods were filled with Stuart's men, so they quickly threw down their weapons. Single-handedly, Stuart captured forty-nine men, including a lieutenant and a surgeon, of the 15th Pennsylvania Infantry.

The skirmish at Falling Waters ended when the Union forces settled back into Martinsburg. At the end of the battle, the Confederate losses were thirteen men killed or missing and twelve wounded. Six Union soldiers were dead, eighteen were wounded, and one man was missing.[7] After the battle, Jackson had nothing but praise for Stuart's accomplishments. Within a short time, Stuart was promoted to the rank of colonel.

Battle of Manassas

The first major battle of the Civil War took place shortly after the encounter at Falling Waters. On July 16, 1861, the Union Army marched out of Washington, D.C., and crossed the Potomac River. Under the command of General Irvin McDowell, thirty-five thousand volunteer soldiers marched into Virginia. Their goal was to destroy the railroad at Manassas Junction and then continue south to capture the Confederate capital at Richmond, Virginia. They hoped to end the war in a week.

Inexperienced Armies
General McDowell was reluctant to take his untrained troops into battle. When he asked for more time to train his men, President Abraham Lincoln commented on the inexperience of both armies, saying, "You are green, it is true; but they [the Confederate troops] are green also. You are all green alike."[8]

With only twenty thousand men General P.G.T. Beauregard stood in the Union Army's way. As soon as he was informed by a Confederate spy that McDowell's forces were advancing, Beauregard asked Richmond for reinforcements. General Johnston's troops were ordered to come down from the Shenandoah Valley and join Beauregard. Stuart and his cavalry screened Johnston's departure so that the Union forces in the valley could not tell they had left.

After Johnston's departure, Stuart was not content to stay in the valley. He left a small number of his men at Charles Town to watch the Union Army's movements in the valley. With four companies, approximately three hundred men, he set out for Manassas Junction on July 19. The roads were so crowded with soldiers and guns that Stuart and his men had to ride through fields. The fences and

ditches greatly slowed their progress and at night they had to be careful not to trample soldiers who had left the roadways for a few hours of rest in the open fields.

On the evening of July 20, thirty-six hours after departing the valley, they arrived in Manassas. They settled down for the night in an open field between Manassas and the Stone Bridge where the Warrenton Road crosses a small stream called Bull Run. Early in the morning Stuart awoke to the sound of distant cannon fire. The battle had begun. Restlessly Stuart and his men waited and watched. Finally, at two o'clock that afternoon, when it appeared the Confederate troops were about to give way, their orders arrived. A courier delivered the message: "Colonel Stuart, General Beauregard directs that you bring your command into action at once and that you attack where the firing is hottest."[9]

The bugle call of "Boots and Saddles" was sounded. The troopers tightened their saddles, adjusted their horses' reins, and mounted. They rode off to battle in columns of fours. On their way to the battlefield, they rode through a field hospital filled with wounded. Amputated arms and legs were piled high to one side near the surgeons' tables. Men in various degrees of agony were lying everywhere. Many of the troopers leaned over in their saddles and vomited.[10]

When they reached the battlefield, the first set of troops they encountered was a regiment of Zouaves—soldiers dressed in French infantry uniforms that consisted of red caps, blue jackets, and baggy red trousers. "Don't run boys. We're here," Stuart told them.[11] After looking more closely at the Zouaves, Stuart asked his aide, "Blackford, are those our men or the enemy?"[12]

Blackford replied, "I don't know. I heard Beauregard brought up some Zouaves from New Orleans."[13] A few seconds later the Zouaves' battle flag flew open in the breeze. They were Union soldiers. Stuart spread his men out in a battle line and ordered them to charge.

The Zouaves fired at Stuart's troops and there were a few casualties. Then the strength of Stuart's column hit, and cut the Zouaves to bits. Red uniforms covered the battlefield. Stuart's men charged a second time as the Zouaves

Soldiers dressed in a uniform typical of the French infantry fought on both sides of the Civil War.

began to retreat. Other Union soldiers joined them as they ran. Out of his five hundred troops, Stuart lost only nine men and eighteen horses.[14]

The battle continued back and forth for most of the day. When Johnston received reinforcements, McDowell realized the battle was lost. He ordered his men to retreat. They left the field in an orderly fashion until the Confederates pursued them. Then panic set in and they, along with a large group of spectators who had come out to see the battle, flooded the roadways back to Washington.

Most of the credit for the Confederate victory at the First Battle of Manassas went to General Thomas Jackson. By holding his ground on Henry House Hill, he earned the nickname "Stonewall" and helped turn the tide of the battle in favor of the South. However, Stuart's men protected Jackson's flank until he could be reinforced by Jubal A. Early's troops.[15] Early later wrote that "Stuart did as much towards saving the battle of First Manassas as any subordinate who participated in it; and yet he has never received any credit for it, in the official reports or otherwise."[16]

After the Battle of Manassas, Stuart developed a unit of light horse artillery. The smaller guns, attached to wagons drawn by horses, could move swiftly and outrace the enemy to high ground whenever it was necessary. To command his new unit he recruited

Thomas Jackson earned the nickname "Stonewall" during the First Battle of Manassas when General Barnard Bee said to his troops, "There is Jackson standing like a stone wall."

twenty-three-year-old John Pelham, a recent graduate of West Point. Pelham had a "boyish appearance" and was "as modest as a maiden in the social circle."[17] The masterly manner in which Pelham handled a battery of guns in the Battle of Manassas had impressed Stuart.[18]

Stuart took his men to Fairfax Court House for a few days after the Battle of Manassas and then set up his headquarters at Munson's Hill. From the hill he could actually see Washington, D.C. He expected the Union Army to attack again, but they never came. Flora came to visit him, but Stuart spent most of his time riding between the picket lines where his troops were on guard duty around the Confederate encampments. One of his men wrote, "Stuart sleeps every night on Munson's Hill without even a blanket under or over him. . . . never resting, always vigilant, always active."[19]

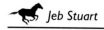

On August 10, 1861, General Johnston, who wanted more cavalry assigned to his army, wrote to Confederate President Jefferson Davis recommending Stuart for a promotion.

A month later on September 24, 1861, Stuart was promoted to the rank of brigadier general and given the command of six regiments of horsemen under General Johnston. Johnston wanted to be the first to inform Flora Stuart, so he sent her a note addressed to "Mrs. Brigadier-General J.E.B. Stuart" and asked if he could carry a message for her to her newly promoted husband.[20]

During the fall and winter of 1861, Stuart established a base camp in a farmhouse halfway between Fairfax Court House and Centreville in Virginia. He called his new camp Qui Vive—French for "Who goes there?"[21] In front of the headquarters sat a Blakely cannon imported from England. Guarding

A Trunk Full of Letters

Stuart had a devilish streak in him. One day he captured a Union officer's trunk and found letters from the officer's wife and the officer's mistress. He suspected that the wife knew nothing of the mistress, so he sent her all the letters. One of Stuart's aides surmised that there would soon be trouble in that family.[22]

the cannon was a huge raccoon chained to the gun carriage. When anyone approached, the raccoon snarled.

Stuart's command now consisted of fifteen hundred men. It was their responsibility to be the eyes and the ears of the Confederate Army. They were constantly on picket duty and probing the enemy lines. At one point Stuart even advised them to enlist the aid of women whenever they could. From the information they obtained, Stuart was able to keep his commander informed about the movements of Union troops around Washington.

Life at camp Qui Vive was not all work. Stuart loved music and several musicians joined his staff. Sam Sweeney, a banjo player, often rode with Stuart. As they rode along, Sweeney would strum the banjo and Stuart would sing. Stuart's favorite songs included "The Dew Is On the Blossom," "Sweet Evelina," and "The Bugle Sang Truce."[23] Stuart also enjoyed playing with his two dogs, Nip and Tuck. Sometimes he would lay them over his saddle and take them with him on horseback.[24]

One day, Stuart's troops captured a Union captain and took him back to their headquarters for questioning. Stuart asked him why his men did not engage in battle more often. The Union officer replied that they had been badly trained and were not very good horse soldiers, but they would be

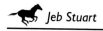

getting better. When Stuart asked why, he was told that his father-in-law, General Philip St. George Cooke, was now commanding the Union cavalry in the area.

That fact that his father-in-law had remained in the Union Army irritated Stuart. In a letter to his brother-in-law, John R. Cooke, Stuart wrote that his father-in-law would regret his decision not to join the Confederacy. He also wrote to Flora, asking her to change their son's name. He had been named Philip St. George Cooke Stuart after Flora's father. In time, Flora complied and renamed him James Ewell Brown Stuart, Jr. Stuart called him Jimmy.

During the long winter of 1862, Stuart grew impatient waiting for the Union Army to advance. President Lincoln had turned command of the Union Army over to General George McClellan, and on December 4, Stuart wrote, "We still expect McClellan daily. That he will advance there can be little doubt, but when and where . . ."[25]

THE
BATTLEFIELD
IN 1862

Mcclellan finally began his Peninsular Campaign in the spring of 1862. Instead of taking his army over land, he floated his forces down the Potomac River to Fort Monroe on the tip of the Virginia Peninsula and then began his slow, cautious march toward Richmond.

With the information Stuart provided General Lee from his ride around McClellan's army, Lee felt confident enough to implement a bold plan. He would bring Stonewall Jackson's troops down from the Shenandoah Valley to join three other Confederate divisions. As soon as Jackson arrived

Composition of Union and Confederate Armies
McClellan's army was organized in corps. Each corps contained twenty thousand men. The Confederate Army was made up of regiments, brigades, and divisions. A regiment could contain from two hundred to one thousand men. Two to six regiments composed a brigade and two or more brigades made up a division. The Confederate Army also had corps, but it was less regimented in its organization.

they would attack the unprotected right flank of McClellan's army. This would leave only two Confederate divisions, about twenty-five thousand men, to guard Richmond.[1] It was a risky maneuver, but Lee reasoned that McClellan would do an "about-face from Richmond" and focus on saving his supply lines.[2]

Seven Days' Battle

Stuart received marching orders late in the evening of June 25, 1862. He was to screen Jackson's movements down from the Shenandoah Valley in Northern Virginia. He met Jackson the following day near Ashland, a village located sixteen miles from Richmond. With Stuart were two thousand horsemen and Pelham's artillery.

Jackson was delighted to see Stuart.[3] He rode over to the side of the road to talk with him. Stuart's fame had spread throughout the South and Jackson's men cheered him and their commander as they marched by.

The contrast between the two men's appearances was striking. Jackson rode a rather sorry-looking horse and wore "a threadbare, faded, semi-military suit, with a disreputable old Virginia Military Institute cap drawn down over his eyes."[4] Stuart's mount was a splendid thoroughbred and he was dressed impeccably in his uniform coat, "yellow sash, highly polished cavalry boots, pistol, and saber."[5]

After their meeting, Stuart continued to scout ahead of Jackson's army and to screen his left flank. Stuart reported "constant skirmishing" with the Union cavalry along his route.[6]

As Jackson slowly marched southward, the rest of the Confederate Army converged on McClellan's right flank at Mechanicsville, Virginia. On the afternoon of June 26, at 3:00 P.M., they grew tired of waiting for Jackson and began their assault. It was a disastrous maneuver. They were driven back and suffered heavy casualties. Out of the 16,356 Confederate soldiers who fought in the battle, 1,484 were lost. The Union casualties were far less.

Out of the 15,631 Union soldiers who fought in the battle, there were only 361 casualties.

Jackson never did arrive on the battlefield that afternoon. After traveling fifteen miles, he ordered his men to set up camp for the night at Hundley's Corner. He was only three miles from the battle. Stuart's horsemen spent the night on picket duty protecting Jackson's camp.

During the night, the Union Army retreated from Mechanicsville and dug trenches to hide in at Gaines's Mill. The following day, Jackson continued to move slowly. The swampy terrain, the heat, and the roads that twisted and turned—sometimes leading nowhere—greatly slowed his progress. Late that afternoon, he arrived at the Battle of Gaines's Mill in time to turn the tide of the battle in favor of the South. The battle lasted seven hours and was a Confederate victory. However, Jackson's men suffered greatly that day. Of the estimated eight thousand Confederate casualties, nearly half were from Jackson's divisions.[7]

At this point, McClellan abandoned his advance on Richmond and began to retreat down the James River. The next morning, June 28, Stuart was ordered to disrupt the Union supply lines as McClellan retreated. Stuart cut telegraph wires and tore up the tracks of the York River Railroad. Then he decided to go down the road to McClellan's main supply base, a plantation called White House. White House had previously been the home of Rooney Lee, the son of General Lee, but was now occupied by Union troops.

Stuart wanted to find out how many Union soldiers were stationed at McClellan's supply base and drive them out if possible. He encountered little resistance on his route. Whenever Union pickets were spotted, they fled as soon as they saw the Confederate horsemen.

The Union Army appeared to be retreating in great numbers. That night, the Union soldiers set fire to their own supply base and the sky was lit up by the fires. It was as bright as day for miles as "vast clouds of smoke rose hundreds of feet in air, and explosions of shells and other ammunition" sounded like a battle.[8]

Stuart obtained information from Union prisoners that five thousand Union soldiers guarded the burning supply depot. Because he was greatly outnumbered, he paraded his dismounted horsemen in view of the Union troops in an attempt to convince them that he had a large infantry attachment with him. He also had his artillery officer John Pelham fire guns from various positions to create the impression that he was accompanied by several artillery divisions. The ruse worked. During the night, boats carried off the Union soldiers who had been protecting the supply depot.

At daylight on June 29, Stuart moved within a quarter of a mile of the smoking ruins of the White House plantation and discovered a Union gunboat, the U.S.S. *Marblehead,* tied up at the docks. He sent seventy-five men and one of Pelham's guns to expose the gunboat. A short battle took place until Pelham's artillery chased the boat away. Stuart watched the whole affair and found it entertaining. It was the first time he had ever heard of a cavalry unit taking on a gunboat and defeating it.[9]

Stuart stayed at the White House planation until July 1, when he received orders from General Lee to rejoin Jackson's troops. He spent the day trying to locate Jackson and missed the fierce Battle of Malvern Hill. The last of the Seven Days' Battles, Malvern Hill was also the most costly for the Confederacy. They suffered the loss of 5,355 men and did not gain an inch of ground. The Union Army lost 3,214 men in the battle.

Stuart favored mounting another attack, but General Lee decided against it. He was sure that McClellan's army no longer posed a threat to Richmond. Also, his men needed time to rest and recover after a week of continual fighting. Stuart's men screened the withdrawal of the Confederate troops. This prevented the Union Army from detecting their movements.

A large number of men were lost by both armies during the Seven Days' Battle. The Confederate Army lost sixteen thousand men, and the Union Army, twenty thousand.[10]

Second Battle of Manassas

After McClellan's poor showing in the Peninsular Campaign, President Lincoln decided to reorganize the Union Army. He consolidated the armies of Major General Nathaniel Banks, General John Charles Frémont, and General Irvin McDowell into the Army of Virginia, and gave Major General John Pope command of the new army.

With his pompous attitude, Pope made himself unpopular with his men and Virginia civilians grew to hate him. He permitted his soldiers to seize food and supplies from Virginia farms without paying for them. He also threatened to hang, without a trial, anyone he suspected of aiding the Confederacy.

Lee considered Pope an evil man who needed to be opposed.[11] If McClellan's army managed to join Pope's troops in northern or central Virginia, Lee would face almost unbeatable odds. Pope had to be stopped before he received reinforcements.

Lee divided his army into two commands and sent Jackson to engage Pope. Stuart's cavalry was to

lead the advance across the Rapidan River. On the night of August 17, Pope's troops captured Stuart's adjutant general, Major Norman R. Fitzhugh, who was carrying a signed copy of Lee's plan of attack.

That evening Stuart was almost captured, too. He was napping on the porch of a farmhouse near Verdiersville, Virginia, waiting for Fitzhugh, when Union horsemen arrived on the scene. He barely had time to mount his horse and head for the woods. To his humiliation, the Union horsemen confiscated his hat and other personal belongings. In a letter to his wife Stuart wrote, "I intend to make the Yankees pay dearly for that hat."[12]

The opportunity to revenge his loss occurred on August 22, when Stuart raided Pope's headquarters at Catlett's Railroad Station. With fifteen hundred horsemen, he swept into the Union camp and took a payroll safe containing half a million dollars, a notebook filled with information about the location and disposition of the Union forces, and Pope's dress coat.

Stuart was delighted with his prize and sent the following letter to General Pope: "You have my hat and plume. I have your best coat. I have the honor to propose a cartel [agreement] for the fair exchange of the prisoners."[13] Pope did not reply. Stuart sent Pope's coat to Richmond where the governor put it on display in the state library.

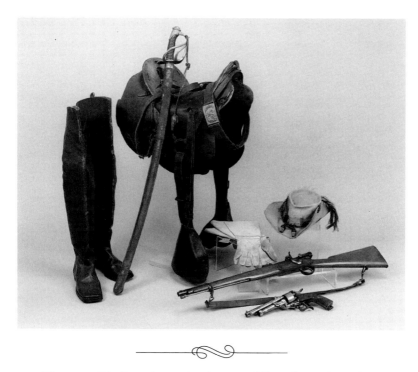

These are Jeb Stuart's cavalry boots, saddle, saber, white gloves, plumed hat, rifle, and pistol.

By August 29, Pope had been driven north by the Confederate Army and was facing Lee's troops. Lee attempted another daring maneuver and sent Stonewall Jackson with his twenty-five thousand troops on a fifty-six–mile march around Pope's army. In two days' time, Jackson was able to sever Pope's connection to the Washington railroad and loot his supply depot at Manassas Junction. Then Jackson entrenched his men on the ridge overlooking the Manassas battlefield. It was the same

battlefield where he had earned his nickname "Stonewall" Jackson the year before.

Pope turned his troops to face Jackson's advance and proclaimed that he would "bag the whole crowd."[14] The battle raged for two days. When Jackson's troops received reinforcements, five divisions under the command of Major General James Longstreet, Pope's men were finally beaten back. The Confederates had won, but both armies had lost nearly 20 percent of their men. Pope lost 16,054 of his 75,696 men, and Lee lost 9,197 of his 48,527 men.[15] Two days after the Second Battle of Manassas, General McClellan once again took command of the Union Army. President Lincoln sent Pope to Minnesota to put down an Indian uprising.

Bloody Maryland

Desperately in need of food and supplies for his army, Lee decided to invade the North in the fall of 1862 and move his army into Maryland. He knew that Virginia could no longer supply his troops and he wanted to relieve the pressure on Richmond. He hoped that the people of Maryland would be sympathetic to the Southern cause and rise up and join him. As his soldiers marched across the Potomac River, they sang "Maryland, My Maryland."

Unfortunately, the Marylanders disappointed Lee. They stayed behind their closed doors and simply watched as his men marched by. One Maryland woman commented, "O, they are so dirty! I don't think the Potomac River could wash them clean. And ragged! There is not a scarecrow in the cornfields that would not scorn to exchange clothes with them. . . ."[16]

Another Marylander, a twelve-year-old boy, thought Lee's men looked like "a hungry set of wolves."[17] Still, he was impressed with the riding skills of Stuart's troopers and thought they rode "like circus riders."[18]

Stuart's cavalry was assigned guard duty over a twenty-mile front across Maryland, east of Lee's army. When McClellan's army marched out of Washington in pursuit of the Confederates, it was the cavalry's job to hold them off as long as possible and report back to Lee regarding their strength, location, and intentions.

Lee sent Jackson's army to secure his communication lines between Richmond and the Shenandoah Valley by taking over Harpers Ferry. Longstreet's divisions were spread out all over western Maryland, and Lee needed time to unite his forces before confronting the Union Army.

Cautiously, McClellan pursued the Southern forces into Maryland. By a quirk of fate, he acquired a copy of the Confederate orders for the Maryland campaign—Lee's Special Order No. 191. In a meadow

where Confederate soldiers had previously camped, a Union private found the orders wrapped around three cigars. The information was quickly taken to Union headquarters. McClellan thought it might be a trap. He waited sixteen hours before he advanced toward Lee's army.

That night, Stuart had a mysterious visitor, a Southern sympathizer, who told him that the Union Army had Lee's orders for the campaign.[19] Stuart quickly reported this information to General Lee. McClellan's hesitation gave Lee time to position his nineteen thousand men on the crest of a four-mile ridge east of Sharpsburg, Maryland, beside a creek called Antietam.

McClellan approached the town of Sharpsburg on September 15, 1862, but waited two days before he attacked. The battle that began on September 17 was the "bloodiest single day of the war."[20] The Union forces consisted of seventy thousand men.

Battle Names

In the South, battles were named after towns, and in the North, they were named after landmarks such as a creek or river. So, in the South this battle was called the Battle of Sharpsburg, and in the North, the Battle of Antietam.

The Confederate forces, many of whom had just arrived, consisted of thirty-nine thousand men.[21]

Even though the Union forces outnumbered the Confederates, they attacked in stages—one corps at a time. Through each attack the Confederates were able to hold their ground. At one point, Stuart's troopers sent their mounts to the rear so they could fight more effectively alongside the infantry.

It was a blood bath. Dead and dying soldiers, from both sides, covered the battlefield. A nearby farm road was piled fifteen feet deep with bodies and would be remembered as "Bloody Lane." There were more than 26,000 casualties that day—13,700 Confederates and 12,350 Union soldiers were dead, wounded, or missing.[22]

McClellan hesitated again and did not attack the next day. This gave Lee time to escape across the Potomac into Virginia. McClellan followed, but not close enough to engage him in battle again.

Chambersburg Raid

After the Battle of Antietam, Jefferson Davis, the Confederate president, was concerned about the safety of Richmond. He feared that McClellan would attempt another campaign before winter. In order to determine McClellan's intentions, Lee once again sent his cavalry commander on a daring raid.

On October 8, 1862, Lee ordered Stuart to take a raiding party across the Potomac River at Williamsport, Virginia. Then he was to proceed to Chambersburg, Pennsylvania, and destroy the railroad bridge over the Conococheague Creek. Stuart was instructed to "inflict upon the enemy" any damage that he could and to obtain information on the "position, force, and probable intention of the enemy."[23] Stuart was also given permission to seize horses.

Confederate horsemen supplied their own mounts. If a trooper's horse were killed in battle or disabled, he had to return home to obtain a new horse. Before long, horses were in short supply and had to be confiscated wherever they could be found.

From each of his three brigades, Stuart chose six hundred men to join the expedition. His artillery commander, Pelham, and four of his guns were to accompany them. At dawn on October 10, Stuart's eighteen hundred horsemen rode across the Potomac River. Stuart assigned two hundred men from each brigade to visit farms along the way and seize horses.

It was a dark and cloudy day and by evening rain began to fall. At seven o'clock, the horsemen reached the outskirts of Chambersburg. They had traveled forty miles and were in the middle of Union territory, but they encountered little opposition.

Stuart seized the town and sent a group of his men to destroy the bridge over the Conococheague Creek. The structure, however, was built of iron and could not be burned down or demolished by axes. In time the men gave up. Before they left, they burned the town's depots, machine shops, stores of military supplies, and a warehouse of ammunition.

On the morning of October 11, Stuart directed his men east out of Chambersburg, toward Gettysburg, Pennsylvania. Once again he decided to do the unexpected and ride around McClellan's army. Stuart's column stretched for almost five miles. Three scouts rode one hundred fifty yards ahead of the advance guard. Two hundred yards behind the advance guard rode six hundred horsemen and an artillery section. In the middle of the procession were six hundred troopers leading about twelve hundred captured horses. Following the horse leaders were six hundred more horsemen and a contingent of artillery. Then came the rear guard followed by three scouts.

Stuart rode with the advance guard and kept his couriers busy, riding up and down the line delivering his instructions. At one point he ordered, "Slow the gait for nothing, and ride over anything that gets in the way."[24]

At Cashtown the column turned south and traveled to Emmitsburg, Maryland. From there they

continued south and rode through Rocky Ridge, Woodsboro, Liberty, New London, New Market, Hyattstown, Barnesville, and Poolesville. On October 12, they crossed the Potomac and entered Leesburg, Virginia. They had traveled 126 miles and they had covered the last 80 miles of their route in 36 hours without stopping.

Once again Stuart had embarrassed the Union Army and its commander with a surprise raid. When President Lincoln was asked about McClellan's failure, Lincoln replied, "When I was a boy we used to play a game, . . . 'Three Times Round, and Out.' Stuart has been round him twice. If he goes around him once more, . . . McClellan will be out."[25]

On November 3, 1862, Stuart's five-year-old daughter, Flora, died. A few days after her death, a telegram arrived at Stuart's headquarters to inform him of her passing. One of his aides awoke him in the middle of the night with the sad news. Stuart read the telegram and his eyes filled with tears. "I will never get over it—never," he later told a friend.[26]

Fredericksburg

After the Chambersburg raid, Stuart established his headquarters, Camp No Camp, about five miles outside of Fredericksburg, on Telegraph Road. From there, Stuart's three brigades of horsemen spread

out for fifty miles along the Rappahannock River,
above and below Fredericksburg.

President Lincoln did not wait for Stuart to ride
around McClellan a third time. On November 5, he
replaced McClellan with General Ambrose E.
Burnside. Burnside quickly took hold of the situation
and moved his army to the outskirts of Fredericksburg.
He planned to cross the Rappahannock River, take
the town, and move on to Richmond.

The bridges across the Rappahannock had been
destroyed, and Burnside had to wait seventeen days
for pontoon bridges to arrive to ferry his one hundred
twenty thousand men across the river. This gave the
Confederate Army time to evacuate Fredericksburg
and position seventy-eight thousand soldiers in the
hills surrounding the town. Lee ordered the town to
be evacuated due to the pending battle.

Watching the townspeople leave was an agoniz-
ing sight for the Confederate soldiers. One
Southern artilleryman said, "I never saw a more piti-
ful procession than they made trudging through the
deep snow . . . little children tugging along with
their doll babies . . . women so old and feeble that
they could carry nothing and could barely hobble
themselves."[27]

At daylight on December 11, Burnside's artillery
began shelling Fredericksburg at a rate of one hundred rounds per minute. By the end of the day, the

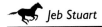

town had been turned into rubble and the Union infantry began to cross the river. The Confederates watched and waited.

On the morning of December 13, Burnside's men attacked. The Union soldiers advanced twelve times, and each time the Confederates held their ground. Stuart later called the Battle of Fredericksburg a "tremendous slaughter."[28] The Union Army lost approximately twelve thousand men and the Confederates about five thousand.[29]

The following day, neither side renewed the battle. Burnside wanted to attack again but his staff persuaded him not to. On December 15 a truce was called to permit both sides to bury their dead. That evening, under the cover of fog, Burnside withdrew his troops across the river. It was a shattering defeat for the North.

8

THE BATTLEFIELD IN 1863

Stuart returned to his headquarters, Camp No Camp, after the Battle of Fredericksburg. The weather turned cold and miserable. Stuart's wife, Flora, came to visit, and Stuart celebrated Christmas with his family and friends. During their visit Flora became pregnant again.

In the months that followed, Stuart went on several information-gathering missions to learn what he could about Burnside's army and to disrupt Burnside's communication and supply lines. During one raid, Stuart took time to complain to the Union quartermaster about the quality of mules he had confiscated. Before destroying the telegraph wires

at Burke's Station on the Orange and Alexandria Railroad, he sent the following telegraph to the United States Quartermaster, United States Army, General Montgomery Meigs:

> *Quality of mules lately furnished me very poor. Interferes seriously with movement of captured wagons.*
>
> *J.E.B. Stuart*[1]

In a confrontation a few months later, Stuart lost his beloved artillery commander. Major John Pelham was mortally wounded in the back of the head by an artillery shell. Stuart cried when he saw his friend's body. He ordered his men to wear a black mourning cloth around their left arms, close to their hearts, and he renamed his headquarters Camp Pelham.

On January 26, 1863, due to Ambrose E. Burnside's poor performance at the Battle of Fredericksburg, President Lincoln replaced him with Major General Joseph Hooker. For the

Major John Pelham, Stuart's favorite artillery officer, was nicknamed "The Gallant Pelham."

next three months, Hooker went about reorganizing and equipping his army. He also revamped the Union cavalry. By spring, he had one hundred thirty thousand men at his disposal and President Lincoln ordered him to destroy Lee's army.

Chancellorsville

Hooker planned an outflanking maneuver. Leaving part of his troops at Fredericksburg, he marched the rest of his army up and across the Rappahannock River, then moved quickly through a thick forest called the Wilderness. He set up his headquarters in the Chancellor House. The house was located on the edge of the Wilderness, near a place where several roads intersected called Chancellorsville.

Hooker's maneuvers did not fool General Lee. He divided his forces and met the Union advance at Chancellorsville. When the Confederates arrived, the Union troops engaged them in battle. Although the battle was going well, Hooker ordered his men back into position near the Chancellor House shortly after the battle began. When Hooker was asked what happened to him at Chancellorsville, he said, "Well, to tell the truth, I just lost confidence in Joe Hooker."[2]

That evening, Lee and Jackson sat on old cracker boxes and warmed their hands by a campfire while they tried to come up with a plan. "How can

we get at these people?"[3] Lee asked. They decided that if they could find a secure route, they would send Jackson's troops to attack Hooker's forces from the rear at Chancellorsville. Stuart was sent to find a road wide enough to accommodate artillery and also to find a local resident to act as their guide.

It was a daring plan, for it left Lee only fourteen thousand men to hold off Hooker's force of fifty thousand. At 5:00 A.M. on May 2, 1863, Jackson and his entire corps of twenty-eight thousand men began their twelve-mile march through the Wilderness, around the Union Army's right flank. Stuart's cavalry led the column.

Two hours before sunset they attacked. Hooker's men were taken completely by surprise. They panicked and ran. One of the Union soldiers remarked afterward that "It was a perfect whirlwind of men. The enemy seemed to come from every direction."[4]

That evening, while scouting for a night attack, Jackson was accidentally shot and wounded by his own troops. His left arm had to be amputated. A. P. Hill, Jackson's second in command, was also seriously wounded. Stuart was summoned to take over Jackson's troops.

When the sun rose the following day, Stuart launched a second attack. His horse, Chancellor, was shot and killed beneath him. He obtained another horse. Then he rode into a Southern regiment that had given way under a Union advance, grabbed their flag, and rallied the men behind him.

One of his aides later wrote, "Stuart was all activity, and wherever the danger was greatest there was he to be found . . . and in the midst of the hottest fire I heard him, to an old melody, hum the words, 'Old Joe Hooker, get out of the Wilderness.'"[5]

Hooker continued to abandon positions and refused to send reinforcements to his men when they were needed. Finally, after being wounded by a Confederate artillery shell, he ordered his men to fall back. On May 6, his army retreated across the Rappahannock. Hooker lost seventeen thousand men in the battle. Lee, however, paid a high price for his victory at Chancellorsville. He lost thirteen thousand men in the battle, and on May 10, Stonewall Jackson died of pneumonia, a complication resulting from his bullet wound.

Because of the loss of Stonewall Jackson, General Lee reorganized the Army of Northern Virginia into three corps. The I Corps was commanded by James Longstreet, whom Lee called "my old war horse."[6] The II Corps, made up of Stonewall Jackson's former troops, was given to Richard S. Ewell, who had served under Jackson in the Shenandoah Campaign. Ewell had lost one of his legs on the battlefield the year before and had to be

strapped into his saddle in order to ride with his troops. The III Corps was commanded by A. P. Hill. A restless and impulsive soldier, Hill had helped win Confederate victories at the Second Battle of Manassas, Fredericksburg, and Chancellorsville.

Concerned about the strength of the newly organized Union cavalry, Lee consolidated his horsemen, nearly ten thousand men, under Stuart. Then he instructed Stuart to "get your cavalry together, and give them breathing time, so as when you do strike," the Union cavalry will feel it.[7]

Culpeper Court House

Stuart assembled his troops at his headquarters near Culpeper Court House in Virginia. When they were rested and drilled to his satisfaction, he decided to display his forces and hold a review. Invitations were issued from Stuart's headquarters and people, mostly ladies, came from far and wide to see the show. General Lee was unable to attend, but former Confederate Secretary of War George Wythe Randolph arrived in a special train with Stuart's battle flag mounted on the front.

At 8:00 A.M. on the morning of June 5, Stuart assembled his horsemen in a line almost two miles long on a level plain near Brandy Station. In the center of the plain was a small hill that served as a reviewing area. For show, Stuart rode to the end of the reviewing line and then back to the hill. As he passed his officers, one by one, they joined him. They rode to the reviewing area and then the squadrons of horsemen rode past them. Three bands played and the horses pranced in time to the music. After completing the full circle, the cavalry rode around again at a faster pace. When they were one hundred yards from the review area, they galloped at full speed past the reviewers, yelling and waving their sabers above their heads as they would in a real battle. While the cavalry charged, the horse artillery fired in the air. One of Stuart's soldiers called it "one of the grandest scenes I ever saw."[8]

Across the Rappahannock, General Hooker was worried. Every day in early June, he sent his orange observation balloons up to spy on Lee's troops. Hooker reported to President Lincoln that new divisions had joined Lee and that Stuart had assembled a tremendous cavalry force near Culpeper. He suspected the Confederate Army would soon be on the move, perhaps to make an invasion of the North.

Hooker was right. In order to relieve Richmond, Lee was preparing to invade the North. His goal was the rich farmlands of Pennsylvania where his army could live off the land. He hoped that a Confederate victory in the North would push England and France into formally recognizing the Confederacy. Also, if he captured a few major Northern cities, maybe

frightened civilians would force their government to negotiate a peace settlement.

Lee ordered Stuart's cavalry to screen the infantry's movements so that their departure would not be detected. On June 7, Lee sent word to Stuart that he would be happy to review his troops before they left on their mission. The next day Stuart's men assembled for another review. This time it was less formal and only attended by the military.

Brandy Station

That night, Stuart packed up his headquarters and made preparations to leave on his mission the following morning. He slept out in the open at Fleetwood Hill near Brandy Station. While he slept, eleven thousand Union horsemen under the command of General Alfred Pleasonton rode across the Rappahannock with orders to find out what Lee was up to and "disperse and destroy" the Confederate forces near Culpeper.[9]

Stuart's cavalry was taken completely by surprise. They were spread out for nearly four miles along the river. Many of the men fought dismounted to give their comrades time to get dressed. Stuart was awakened by the sound of artillery fire but did not know what was going on until couriers reached him. He sent out a flurry of orders, trying to organize his men.

By late morning, the battle was centered around Fleetwood Hill. Stuart's aide, W. W. Blackford, later wrote:

> It was a thrilling sight to see these dashing horsemen draw their sabres and start for the hill . . . at a gallop. . . . The lines met on the hill. . . . acres and acres of horsemen sparkling with sabres . . . hurled against each other at full speed and meeting with a shock that made the earth tremble.[10]

For twelve hours, twenty-one thousand horsemen fought valiantly in the largest cavalry confrontation in American history. Fleetwood Hill changed hands many times during the day. Late that afternoon, Stuart sent a message to General Longstreet requesting assistance. When the Confederate infantry advanced, Pleasonton finally withdrew his troops back across the Rappahannock. But Pleasonton had accomplished his mission. He reported to General Hooker that Lee was leaving Fredericksburg to head north.

The Confederate casualties were 523 men and the Union 936 soldiers.[11] Although technically a Confederate victory, this battle was the first time the Union cavalry had stood up to the Confederate cavalry. From this experience they gained confidence in themselves and their commanders.[12]

Stuart was humiliated by the surprise attack by the Union. A few Southerners wrote letters to President Jefferson Davis complaining that Stuart

was too busy playing and should pay more attention to his duty. The *Examiner*, the Richmond newspaper, scolded Stuart, but his commander, General Lee, never reprimanded him.

Route North

On June 12, three days after the Battle of Brandy Station, Lee's army was spaced out over fifty miles. Ewell was marching toward Winchester and Longstreet's men were in Culpeper. A. P. Hill's troops stayed in Fredericksburg for a time to try to deceive Hooker about Lee's intentions.

Stuart's men were divided among the three corps and assigned to shield the infantry's movements. The Union cavalry tried to penetrate this shield but was beaten back in confrontations at Adlie, Middleburg, and Upperville in Virginia. During these engagements, between June 17 and June 21, 1863, the Union lost 827 men and the Confederacy lost 660 men.

On June 22, Stuart set up his headquarters at Rector's Crossroads, near Middleburg. It was time for Stuart's horsemen to join the main part of Lee's army in Pennsylvania, but he was not sure what route they should take. If they marched down the Shenandoah Valley, west of the Blue Ridge Mountains, they might lead the Union cavalry directly to Lee's army. Stuart wrote to Lee and

Longstreet asking for guidance. Lee suggested he leave two of his brigades at the passes in the Blue Ridge Mountains and start moving north with his other three brigades to join Ewell in Pennsylvania. Longstreet urged Stuart to cross the Potomac in the rear of Hooker's army.

On June 23, Stuart sent out scouts who confirmed that he could cross the Potomac between Hooker's army and Washington, D.C. He hoped this route would confuse the Union command and enable him to raid the Union supply lines. In a message to Lee he outlined his plans and waited for orders.

It rained all day. That evening, Stuart slept under a tree near his headquarters. He felt that his officers should have to endure the same conditions as his troops.[13] In the middle of the night, a courier arrived with Lee's instructions, which said: "You will . . . be able to judge whether you can pass around their army without hindrance, doing them all the damage you can, and cross the river *east of the Mountains*."[14]

The next morning, Stuart made preparations to leave. He ordered two of his brigades to meet up with him at Salem, Virginia, ten miles away. He took six artillery pieces and left the rest for his men to use in guarding the passes through the Blue Ridge Mountains. He ordered the men left behind to harass Hooker's troops as long as they were in Virginia.

At one o'clock in the morning on June 25, Stuart rode out of Salem and headed toward Haymarket. Stuart had two options. He could either take a shorter route that would allow him to meet Lee sooner, or a longer route that would let him do more damage to the Union supply lines. He chose the longer route. Since Lee's orders were not specific as to where he should cross the Potomac, he decided to do as much raiding as he could before he joined Ewell in Pennsylvania.

When he came upon a corps of Union infantry near Haymarket, Stuart altered his course. He allowed his men to feed their horses, and the next day they headed for Wolf Run Shoals on the Occoquan River. On June 27, he marched through Fairfax Court House to Dranesville and on to Rowser's Ford on the Potomac. During his march, Stuart discovered evidence that Hooker's army was moving north. He sent a messenger to find Lee, but the courier never got through.

No Union guards were posted at Rowser's Ford, about twenty miles from Washington, but the Potomac River was very high. Stuart doubted that his guns and ambulances could get across. He sent scouts out to find a safer crossing. None could be found and he was forced to send his men across at Rowser's Ford. It was a difficult crossing, and the men and horses were exhausted by the time they reached the Maryland shore.

The column moved onward to Rockville, about fifteen miles from Washington on the Frederick Road. Stuart's men destroyed telegraph lines and overcame a wagon train of 125 wagons containing oats and whiskey. United States government officials in Washington, D.C., were shocked that Jeb Stuart was raiding under their very noses.[15]

Union General Meade was not sure where Lee was going, and Lee had no idea where the Union Army was located. Lee thought that if Union troops were nearby, Stuart would inform him, so he pushed further north in Pennsylvania.

On June 29, Stuart continued north with his men. The 125 captured wagons greatly slowed his progress. Along the way, his troopers destroyed tracks on the Baltimore and Ohio Railroad and cut

Lincoln Replaces Hooker

Hooker wanted to attack Richmond when he learned that Lee's army was moving north. President Lincoln reminded him that Lee's army, not the Confederate capital, was the goal. Hooker complained that he needed more men and equipment. On June 28, Lincoln replaced him with General George Meade.

telegraph wires. In Westminster, Maryland, they met some opposition, two companies of Delaware cavalry, but pressed on to Union Mills. Stuart had no way of knowing it, but he was almost in the middle of the Union Army as it rode north to find Lee. He had approximately forty-one thousand Union troops ahead of him—between him and Lee's forces—and almost another forty-one thousand Union soldiers behind him.[16]

Carlisle

Stuart collided with a brigade of Union cavalry at Hanover, Maryland, and had to detour further north. At daylight on July 1, his column reached Dover. He still had not located Lee's army and he needed food for his men and horses. He sent out scouts to find Lee. Following a rumor that there might be friendly troops and food in Carlisle, Pennsylvania, he continued northeast.[17]

When the Confederates arrived at Carlisle, they found it occupied by two brigades of Pennsylvania militia. It was clear that if they wanted food, they were going to have to fight for it. Stuart attempted to convince the militia officers to surrender. They refused, so he ordered his artillery to shell the town and had his men burn the United States cavalry barracks nearby.

Gettysburg

Later that night, Stuart's scout returned. Lee was in Gettysburg, thirty-three miles away, and he wanted Stuart to join him. The scout also reported that a great victory over the Union infantry had been won that day.

After the initial confrontation on July 1, both armies continued to gather their troops at Gettysburg until there were sixty-five thousand Confederates facing eighty-five thousand Union soldiers. On July 2, the Union battle line was shaped like a fishhook. The tip of the hook was at Culp's Hill, the hook curved around Cemetery Hill, and the shank ran along Cemetery Ridge. Hills called Big Round Top and Little Round Top were also occupied by Union troops and overlooked the battle line.

Lee's army was stretched around the outside of the hook with Ewell's troops on the north, A. P. Hill's men in the center, and Longstreet's troops to the south. Lee wanted the hills, Big Round Top and Little Round Top, taken. He assigned Longstreet to do the job. It took all morning and most of the afternoon for Longstreet to position his troops. At four o'clock in the afternoon, Longstreet finally attacked. He captured positions known as Peach Orchard, Wheat Field, and Devil's Den, but was unable to seize the vital position he was after, Little Round Top.

Stuart rode ahead of his troops and met Lee late that afternoon of July 2. Lee said angrily, "I have not heard from you for days, and you [are] the eyes and ears of my army."

"I have brought you 125 wagons and their teams, General," Stuart replied.

"Yes," Lee answered, "and they are an impediment to me now." When he saw Stuart's distress he added, "Let me ask your help . . . We will not discuss this matter further. Help me fight these people."[18]

That evening, the Union battle line on the left and right still held. Lee thought that an assault on the center might work the following day. He ordered Stuart to protect the far left flank of the Confederate Army. In mid-afternoon on July 3, the Union cavalry engaged Stuart's horsemen as Lee hurled fifteen thousand soldiers, including General George E. Pickett's brigade, at the center of the Union battle line on Cemetery Ridge. Although led by Longstreet, the attack became known as Pickett's Charge. The Confederate soldiers had to run across an open field and up the hill under constant fire from Union artillery. Many men died before they could reach the Union battle line and all of the Confederates who broke through the battle line were either captured or killed.

The Confederates lost sixty-five hundred men, including fifteen regimental commanders, sixteen

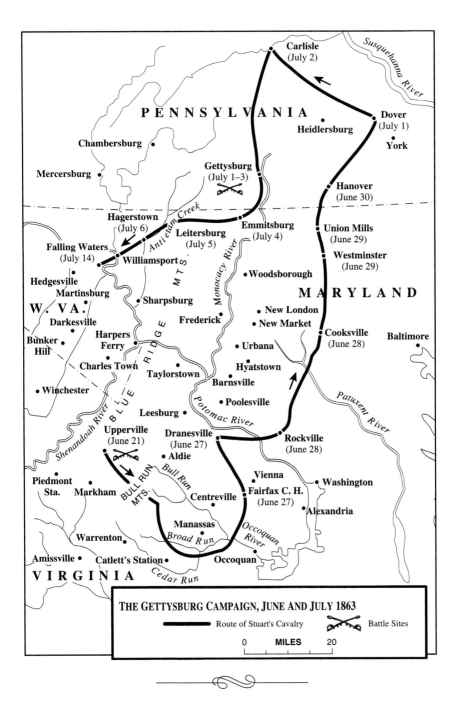

The Gettysburg Campaign, June and July 1863

Route of Stuart's Cavalry — Battle Sites

0   MILES   20

This map shows the route Stuart took as he traveled to meet General Lee during the Gettysburg campaign.

During the Battle of Gettysburg, thousands of Confederates were killed, wounded, or captured. These three Confederate prisoners were captured by Union forces during the battle.

field officers, three brigadier generals, and eight colonels. Every one of the men who composed the University Greys, a company made up of college students from Mississippi, was either killed or wounded.[19]

During three days of fighting, nearly a third of the men engaged in the bloody Battle of Gettysburg—fifty-one thousand men—were either killed, missing, or wounded. The Union Army suffered 23,049 casualties and the Confederate Army, 28,063. On July 4, Lee began his slow retreat back to Virginia. He took with him every gun, wagon, and wounded soldier that could be found. His wagon train stretched seventeen miles.

When his rear guard informed Lee that his troops were all back in Virginia he replied, "Thank God!"[20] Lee blamed himself for the humiliating defeat and tried to resign, but President Davis knew he could not replace him and would not accept his resignation.

Stuart's reputation suffered greatly after the Battle of Gettysburg. Though many people blamed him for the Confederate defeat, others felt he was a scapegoat. He certainly was not the only Confederate officer whose performance was not ideal. Neither Longstreet nor Ewell followed through with Lee's orders in a timely manner during the battle. Many people shared the blame for the Confederate loss.

9

STUART'S LAST BATTLE

On October 9, Stuart's third child, a baby girl, was born. Stuart advised his wife to give their daughter a patriotic name. She named her Virginia after Stuart's beloved home state and gave her the middle name of Pelham in honor of Stuart's late artillery officer, John Pelham.

Although there were many skirmishes between the Confederate and Union armies, no major battles were fought in the fall of 1863. As the weather turned cold, both armies went into winter quarters. Stuart set up his headquarters east of Hanover Court House in Virginia and called it Wigwam. Once again, his family came for Christmas and

Another Jeb Stuart
In early February, someone gave Stuart a special turkey. The bird had dodged innumerable bullets and earned the nickname "Jeb Stuart." Stuart invited General Lee and his staff to join him in a dinner to devour his namesake. Lee declined, saying that he "could not bear to see 'Jeb Stuart' consumed."[1]

stayed in a house nearby. His son Jimmy was three and a half years old and called himself General Jimmy Jeb Stuart, Junior. He liked to roughhouse with his father and run among the horses in the army camp.

Music, as usual, was a big part of camp life at Wigwam. Musicians entertained almost nightly. A sadness fell over the camp when Sam Sweeney, Stuart's beloved banjo player, died of smallpox that winter.

In early March 1864, President Lincoln turned all of the Union armies over to General Ulysses S. Grant. At the time, the Union Army was divided into nineteen departments that acted independently of each other. Grant's plan was to "concentrate all the force possible against the Confederate armies in the field."[2] He planned to strike simultaneous blows against the Confederate Army in the Shenandoah

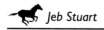

Valley, in Georgia, and in Virginia against Lee's forces.

The Wilderness

Stuart's cavalry was on picket duty along the Rapidan River. Across the river, Grant had one hundred thousand infantry and nearly thirteen thousand horsemen. After midnight on the morning of May 4, pickets sent out the alarm that the "Yankees are crossing, in force."[3]

Determined to sever Lee's lines of communication with Richmond, Grant planned to move through the overgrown forest called the Wilderness into battle positions under the cover of darkness. However, he was unable to get his army through the difficult terrain in one night. Lee had planned to attack that morning, but waited for reinforcements. While Lee was waiting, General Grant's forces made it through the Wilderness and attacked first.

The battle began around noon and turned into total chaos. Units became lost and fired on their own comrades. A Union private remembered:

> No one could see the fight fifty feet from him . . . the lines were very near each other, and from the dense underbrush and the tops of trees came puffs of smoke, the "ping" of the bullets and the yell of the enemy. It was a blind and bloody hunt to the death, in bewildering thickets, rather than a battle.[4]

Because of the density of the Wilderness, cavalry and artillery could not be used effectively. The battle lasted four hours and although Union forces inflicted heavy casualties on the Confederates, they were unable to win the battle. Grant renewed his efforts on the following day, but the battle ended at nightfall without a conclusive outcome. The Union Army lost an estimated 17,666 men, and the Confederates lost 7,750.[5] Instead of retreating, Grant moved south toward Spotsylvania. Lee had predicted General Grant's movement and was waiting for him.

On May 7, Stuart sent Flora a telegram, telling her he was "safe and well."[6] The following day, he helped guide and deploy Confederate troops near Spotsylvania. For a while, he commanded infantry and cavalry troops who had dismounted in a desperate battle to hold Spotsylvania.

Meanwhile, across the battle line in Union headquarters, Philip Sheridan, the commander of Grant's cavalry, lost his temper. He complained to Grant that if he was to fight cavalry, then Grant should let him do his job. He was tired of his men being pulled away to guard wagons or prisoners, or cover picket lines. He wanted to concentrate his entire force and go after Stuart's cavalry.

Grant gave him his blessing and on May 9, Sheridan moved away from the Battle of Spotsylvania and headed south on Telegraph Road. His column of ten thousand troops covered thirteen

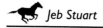

miles of road. Stuart was informed of Sheridan's movements. With three brigades, around forty-five hundred men, Stuart set out after him. He rode throughout the night, following Sheridan's trail south.

At the Beaver Dam Station on the Virginia Central Railroad, the Union troops burned a large amount of rations and medical supplies. They also destroyed two locomotives, one hundred railroad cars, and ten miles of railroad tracks. After regrouping, they headed toward Richmond.

Stuart arrived at Beaver Dam Station shortly after the Union troops left on the morning of May 10. He was concerned about Flora and his children who were staying nearby at the home of Edmund Fontaine. While his men rested, he rode to the Fontaine home to check on his family. He spoke to his wife for few minutes while still mounted on his horse. Then he kissed her good-bye and rode back to his men.

Yellow Tavern

Stuart knew the Union troops were headed for Richmond and set out to beat them to their destination. He rode through most of the day and night. At 10:00 A.M. on May 11, he reached Yellow Tavern, the intersection between Telegraph and Mountain roads, ahead of Sheridan's column. He deployed his men along Mountain Road and waited to surprise Sheridan's troops. He chose to fight dismounted. He felt his men would have a better advantage even though it meant that a quarter of his troops stood away from the battle line, holding their comrades' horses.

Shortly before noon, the Union horsemen rode down Mountain Road. A fierce battle took place. After two hours, there was a lull in the fighting. Then at 4:00 P.M., the Union troops attacked again. Stuart mounted his horse and rode around the battlefield, rallying his men. At one point, a Union soldier ran past him and fired a single shot. The bullet struck Stuart on the right side, just below his ribs. He slumped in his saddle and grabbed his side. Quickly his men came to his assistance. Stuart ordered one of them to go get General Fitzhugh Lee and his staff surgeon.

When Lee arrived, Stuart turned his command over to him, saying "Go ahead, Fitz, old fellow. I know you will do what is right!"[7]

Shortly afterward, the doctor and ambulance arrived. They loaded Stuart into the ambulance and as they left the battlefield, Stuart noticed several Confederate soldiers leaving the area. He yelled at them saying, "Go back! Go back, and do your duty, as I have done mine, and our country will be safe.

Go back! Go back! I had rather die than be whipped. . . ."[8]

As the ambulance jolted along the road, the doctor turned Stuart over to examine his wounds. Stuart looked over at his aide, Walter Hullihen, and calling him by his nickname, asked, "Honey-bun, how do I look in the face?"[9]

"General," Hullihen replied, "you are looking right well. You will be all right."[10]

Fearful that his patient would go into shock, the doctor wanted Stuart to drink some whiskey. Stuart refused because of the vow he had made to his mother when he was a boy. Finally, his aides convinced him to take a few sips.

After dark that evening, they reached Richmond and took Stuart to the home of his brother-in-law, Dr. Charles Brewer. Several doctors examined Stuart and they all agreed that there was nothing they could do for him but apply ice to the wound. A telegraph

This is Major General Jeb Stuart as he looked during the years he led the Confederate cavalry in the Civil War.

message was sent to Flora to come as quickly as possible.

Stuart was in intense pain throughout the night. At noon on the following day, President Jefferson Davis visited him. Taking hold of Stuart's hand, Davis asked, "General, how do you feel?"[11]

Stuart replied, "Easy, but willing to die, if God and my country think I have fulfilled my destiny and done my duty."[12]

Throughout the afternoon, Stuart was delirious. His mind wandered from the battlefield to his family and back again. His pain increased as the day wore on. During the evening, he asked his brother-in-law how long he would live and if he could survive. Brewer answered him calmly but honestly. There was no hope. He could not survive his wounds.

Later in the afternoon, Stuart instructed his aides to take care of his official papers and send all of his personal belongings to Flora. He also requested that his son be given his sword. Then he divided his horses among his men and asked about his wife.

A little after 7:00 P.M., everyone in the room gathered around Stuart's bed while the Reverend Joshua Peterkin prayed. Afterward, they sang Stuart's favorite hymn, "Rock of Ages." Stuart sang along as best he could and then said, "I am going fast now, I am resigned; God's will be done."[14] He

Stuart's Belongings

After Stuart's death, several items were found in his pockets: a thin round pin cushion with Stuart's name embroidered on one side and the Confederate flag on the other, a copy of one of his orders, a commendation congratulating the infantry he commanded at Chancellorsville, a letter to his wife, a poem about the death of a child, a copy of the New Testament, a handkerchief, and a lock of his daughter's hair.

drifted into unconsciousness and died at 7:38 P.M. on Thursday, May 12, 1864, at the age of thirty-one.

Flora arrived at the Brewer home about 11:00 P.M. that night. Due to the battle and the disruption of the railroads, she had spent a traumatic ten-hour journey trying to reach her husband's bedside. A friend who accompanied her wrote, "A certain quiet resting on all about the house instantly impressed them."[15] Words were not necessary to tell them what had happened.[16] When they entered the Brewer home, Flora's children were gently taken from her, and she sat alone in a candlelit room, beside her dead husband.

$$\boxed{10}$$

EPILOGUE

When General Lee learned that Stuart was dying, he said in a shaken voice, "He never brought me a piece of false information."[1] Later, when one of Stuart's officers came to tell him about Stuart's final moments, Lee said, "I can scarcely think about him without weeping!"[2]

Around five o'clock in the afternoon on May 13, 1864, Stuart's funeral was held at St. James Church in Richmond. Cannon fire could be heard in the distance and no military escort was available because of the war. Stuart's troops were unable to attend the service due to the battle raging nearby. Pallbearers

carried Stuart's coffin up the center aisle of the church while the choir sang. Flora sat in the front of the church and wept during the service. President Davis attended, along with Generals Braxton Bragg and Robert Ransom, and other city officials. The Reverend Joshua Peterkin officiated at the service. Afterward, Stuart's coffin was placed in a hearse drawn by four white horses and taken to the Hollywood Cemetery. A short service was performed at his gravesite.

In his will, Stuart requested that his children be educated south of the Mason-Dixon line and that

This is Stuart's gravesite at the Hollywood Cemetery in Richmond.

his family continue to live in the South. Flora's father tried to convince her to come north after Stuart's death. He made arrangements for her to pass through Southern lines, but she refused.

On April 9, 1865, General Lee surrendered to Grant at Appomattox Court House, Virginia. The Civil War had ended. The Union was victorious.

James Ewell Brown Stuart II—originally named Philip St. George Cooke Stuart—followed in his father's and grandfather's footsteps. He joined the United States Army and retired as a captain. In his later years, he lived in New York City.

Virginia Pelham Stuart married Robert Page Waller on November 5, 1887. They lived in Norfolk, Virginia, and Virginia had three children—Flora Stuart Waller, Matthew Page Waller, and Virginia Stuart Waller—before dying in 1898 shortly after childbirth.

For many years after the war, Flora was the principal of an all-girl school, the Virginia Female Institute, in Staunton, Virginia. The school was eventually named Stuart Hall in her honor. After her daughter's death she moved to Norfolk to take care of her son-in-law's family. She remained with them for twenty-five years. Flora died on May 10, 1923, within two days of the fiftieth anniversary of her husband's death. She wore black, mourning his death, for all of those years.

When Stuart died, the South mourned the loss of its "most gallant cavalier."[3] Even a few Northerners commented on his death. Union General John Sedgwick felt that Stuart had been "the greatest cavalry officer ever foaled [born] in America."[4] But General Lee, who loved Stuart like his own son, paid him the most touching tribute, saying: "Among the gallant officers who have fallen in this war, General Stuart was second to none in valor, in zeal, and in unfaltering devotion to his country."[5]

CHRONOLOGY

1833—Born in Patrick County, Virginia, on February 6.

1845—Attends boarding school in Wytheville, Virginia.

1848—Attends Emory & Henry College in Virginia.

1850—Attends the United States Military Academy at West
-1854   Point.

1854—Commissioned a second lieutenant; Reports to Fort Clark
in Laredo, Texas.

1855—Commissioned a second lieutenant in the 1st Cavalry;
Marries Flora Cooke on November 14; Promoted to first
lieutenant on December 20.

1857—Daughter Flora is born in first week of September.

1859—John Brown's raid on Harpers Ferry on October 16.

1860—Son, James Ewell Brown Stuart II, born on June 26.

1861—Resigns commission in United States Army on May 3;
Appointed lieutenant colonel in the Provisional Army of
Virginia on May 10; Promoted to captain in the
Confederate cavalry on May 24; Battle of Falling Waters
on July 2; Promoted to colonel in the cavalry on July 16;
First Battle of Manassas on July 21; Promoted to brigadier
general on September 24.

1862—First ride around McClellan's army on June 12–15;
Promoted to major general on July 25; Seven Days' Battle
on June 25–July 2; Second Battle of Manassas on August
27–30; Battle of Antietam on September 17; Second ride
around McClellan's army on October 9–12; Daughter
Flora dies on November 3; Battle of Fredericksburg on
December 13.

1863—Daughter Virginia born on October 9; Battle of
Chancellorsville on May 2; Battle of Brandy Station on
June 9; Battle of Gettysburg on July 1–3.

1864—Battle of the Wilderness on May 5–7; Shot at Battle of
Yellow Tavern on May 11; Dies on May 12.

Chapter Notes

Chapter 1
1. Geoffrey C. Ward, *The Civil War: An Illustrated History* (New York: Alfred A. Knopf, 1994), p. 110.
2. Ibid.
3. William R. Brooksher and David K. Snider, *Glory at a Gallop: Tales of the Confederate Cavalry* (Washington: Brassey's, 1993), p. 5.
4. Douglas Southall Freeman, *Lee's Lieutenants: A Study in Command, Volume One* (New York: Charles Scribner's Sons, 1944), p. 285.
5. Ibid., p. 289.
6. Burke Davis, *Jeb Stuart: The Last Cavalier* (New York: Holt, Rinehart and Winston, 1957), p. 123.

Chapter 2
1. Emory M. Thomas, "The Real J.E.B. Stuart," *Civil War Times Illustrated*, November/December 1989, p. 35.
2. Emory M. Thomas, *Bold Dragoon: The Life of J.E.B. Stuart* (New York: Harper & Row, Publishers, 1986), p. 8.
3. Thomas, "The Real J.E.B. Stuart," p. 35.
4. Thomas, *Bold Dragoon: The Life of J.E.B. Stuart*, p. 10.
5. Ibid.
6. Ibid., p. 15.
7. Burke Davis, *Jeb Stuart: The Last Cavalier* (New York: Holt, Rinehart and Winston, 1957), p. 19.
8. Ibid.
9. Ibid.
10. Thomas, *Bold Dragoon: The Life of J.E.B. Stuart*, pp. 19–20.
11. Ibid., p. 20.
12. Ibid.
13. Ibid., p. 21.
14. Mark Nesbitt, *Saber and Scapegoat: J.E.B. Stuart and the Gettysburg Controversy* (Mechanicsburg, Pa.: Stackpole Books, 1994), p. 5.
15. Thomas, *Bold Dragoon: The Life of J.E.B. Stuart*, p. 26.
16. Ibid.

17. Davis, p. 22.

Chapter 3

1. Emory M. Thomas, *Bold Dragoon: The Life of J.E.B. Stuart* (New York: Harper & Row, Publishers, 1986), p. 37.

2. Burke Davis, *Jeb Stuart: The Last Cavalier* (New York: Holt, Rinehart and Winston, 1957), p. 31.

3. Ibid., p. 32.

4. Ibid.

5. Ibid.

6. Ibid., p. 33.

7. Ibid.

8. Ibid.

9. Henry B. McClellan, *I Rode with Jeb Stuart* (New York: Da Capo Press, 1994), p. 17.

10. Ibid., p. 14.

11. Ibid.

12. Davis, p. 34.

13. Thomas, p. 42.

14. Davis, p. 37.

15. Thomas, p. 43.

16. Hampden H. Smith, *J.E.B. Stuart, A Character Sketch* (Richmond: Williams Ptg. Co.), p. 23.

17. Thomas, p. 52.

Chapter 4

1. National Park Service, *John Brown's Raid* (U.S. Government Printing Office, 1990), p. 1.

2. Emory M. Thomas, *Bold Dragoon: The Life of J.E.B. Stuart* (New York: Harper & Row, Publishers, 1986), p. 54.

3. National Park Service, *John Brown's Raid*, p. 46.

4. Ibid.

5. Mark Nesbitt, *Saber and Scapegoat: J.E.B. Stuart and the Gettysburg Controversy* (Mechanicsburg, Pa.: Stackpole Books, 1994), p. 13.

Chapter 5

1. Geoffrey C. Ward, *The Civil War: An Illustrated History* (New York: Alfred A. Knopf, 1994), p. 19.

2. Emory M. Thomas, *Bold Dragoon: The Life of J.E.B. Stuart* (New York: Harper & Row, Publishers, 1986), p. 64.

3. Ibid., p. 65.

4. Ibid.

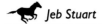

5. Burke Davis, *Jeb Stuart: The Last Cavalier* (New York: Holt, Rinehart and Winston, 1957), p. 46.

6. Shelby Foote, *The Civil War: A Narrative* (New York: Random House, 1958), vol. 1, p. 52.

7. Burke Davis, *They Called Him Stonewall* (New York: Holt, Rinehart & Winston, Inc., 1954), p. 143.

8. Ibid.

Chapter 6

1. Emory M. Thomas, *Bold Dragoon: The Life of J.E.B. Stuart* (New York: Harper & Row, Publishers, 1986), p. 72.

2. Ibid.

3. Ibid.

4. Ibid.

5. Ibid.

6. W. W. Blackford, *War Years with Jeb Stuart* (New York: Charles Scribner's Sons, 1945), p. 16.

7. Lenoir Chambers, *Stonewall Jackson: The Legend and the Man* (New York: William Morrow and Co., 1959), vol. 1, p. 353.

8. Shelby Foote, *The Civil War: A Narrative* (New York: Random House, 1958), vol. 1, p. 71.

9. Blackford, p. 27.

10. Thomas, p. 79.

11. Foote, vol. 1, p. 80.

12. Blackford, p. 28.

13. Burke Davis, *Jeb Stuart: The Last Cavalier* (New York: Holt, Rinehart and Winston, 1957), p. 63.

14. Ibid.

15. Blackford, p. 33.

16. Mark Nesbitt, *Saber and Scapegoat: J.E.B. Stuart and the Gettysburg Controversy* (Mechanicsburg, Pa.: Stackpole Books, 1994), p. 20.

17. Davis, p. 84.

18. Ibid.

19. Thomas, p. 84.

20. Ibid., p. 88.

21. Davis, p. 70.

22. Thomas, p. 90.

23. Davis, p. 88.

24. Fairfax Downey, *Famous Horses of the Civil War* (New York: Thomas Nelson & Sons, 1959), p. 38.

25. Davis, p. 81.

Chapter 7

1. John W. Thomason, *Jeb Stuart* (New York: Charles Scribner's Sons, 1930), p. 167.
2. Richard Wheeler, *Voices of the Civil War* (New York: Meridan, 1990), p. 133.
3. W. W. Blackford, *War Years with Jeb Stuart* (New York: Charles Scribner's Sons, 1945), p. 71.
4. Ibid.
5. Emory M. Thomas, *Bold Dragoon: The Life of J.E.B. Stuart* (New York: Harper & Row, Publishers, 1986), p. 131.
6. Ibid., p. 132.
7. Burke Davis, *Jeb Stuart: The Last Cavalier* (New York: Holt, Rinehart and Winston, 1957), p. 137.
8. Blackford, p. 75.
9. Thomason, p. 199.
10. Richard Wheeler, *Voices of the Civil War* (New York: NAL Dutton, 1990), p. 152.
11. Geoffrey C. Ward, *The Civil War: An Illustrated History* (New York: Alfred A. Knopf, 1994), p. 146.
12. Thomason, p. 225.
13. Shelby Foote, *The Civil War: A Narrative* (New York: Random House, 1958), vol. 1, p. 610.
14. Ward, p. 147.
15. Mark M. Boatner, *The Civil War Dictionary* (New York: Vintage Books, 1991), p. 105.
16. Wheeler, p. 182.
17. Davis, p. 191.
18. Ibid.
19. Ibid., p. 201.
20. Ward, p. 160.
21. Thomas, p. 168.
22. Ibid.
23. Mark Nesbitt, *Saber and Scapegoat: J.E.B. Stuart and the Gettysburg Controversy* (Mechanicsburg, Pa.: Stackpole Books, 1994), p. 30.
24. Davis, p. 227.
25. Foote, vol. 1, p. 751.
26. Thomas, pp. 188–189.
27. Wheeler, p. 206.
28. Thomas, p. 193.
29. Wheeler, p. 219.

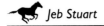

Chapter 8

1. Mark Nesbitt, *Saber and Scapegoat: J.E.B. Stuart and the Gettysburg Controversy* (Mechanicsburg, Pa.: Stackpole Books, 1994), p. 35.

2. Richard Wheeler, *Voices of the Civil War* (New York: Meridan, 1990), p. 276.

3. Douglas Freeman, *Lee: An Abridgement in One Volume*, ed. Richard Harwell (New York: Charles Scribner's Sons, 1961), p. 291.

4. Wheeler, p. 259.

5. Ibid., p. 269.

6. Geoffrey Ward, *The Civil War: An Illustrated History* (New York: Alfred A. Knopf, 1994), p. 214.

7. Emory M. Thomas, *Bold Dragoon: The Life of J.E.B. Stuart* (New York: Harper & Row, Publishers, 1986), pp. 215–216.

8. Ibid., p. 218.

9. Ibid., p. 221.

10. W. W. Blackford, *War Years with Jeb Stuart* (New York: Charles Scribner's Sons, 1945), pp. 215–216.

11. Mark M. Boatner, *The Civil War Dictionary* (New York: Vintage Books, 1991), p. 81.

12. Thomas, p. 226.

13. John W. Thomason, *Jeb Stuart* (New York: Charles Scribner's Sons, 1930), p. 424.

14. Ibid., p. 423.

15. Ibid., p. 429.

16. Thomas, pp. 244–245.

17. Ibid., p. 245.

18. Ward, p. 218.

19. Ibid., pp. 235–236.

20. Thomason, p. 453.

Chapter 9

1. Emory M. Thomas, *Bold Dragoon: The Life of J.E.B. Stuart* (New York: Harper & Row, Publishers, 1986), p. 280.

2. Geoffrey C. Ward, *The Civil War: An Illustrated History* (New York: Alfred A. Knopf, 1994), p. 285.

3. John W. Thomason, *Jeb Stuart* (New York: Charles Scribner's Sons, 1930), p. 486.

4. Ward, p. 288.

5. Mark M. Boatner, *The Civil War Dictionary* (New York: Vintage Books, 1991), p. 925.

6. Thomason, p. 488.

7. Ibid., p. 499.

8. Ibid.

9. Ibid, p. 500.

10. Ibid.

11. Rod Gragg, *The Illustrated Confederate Reader* (New York: Harper & Row, Publishers, 1989), p. 202.

12. Ibid.

13. Ibid., p. 203.

14. Ibid.

15. Burke Davis, *Jeb Stuart: The Last Cavalier* (New York: Holt, Rinehart and Winston, 1957), p. 418.

16. Ibid.

Chapter 10

1. Douglas Southall Freeman, *Lee: An Abridgement in One Volume*, ed. Richard Harwell (New York: Charles Scribner's Sons, 1961), p. 388.

2. Ibid.

3. Emory M. Thomas, "The Real J.E.B. Stuart," *Civil War Times Illustrated*, November/December 1989, p. 34.

4. David Knapp, Jr., *The Confederate Horsemen* (New York: Vantage Press, 1966), p. 37.

5. Ibid., pp. 37–38.

GLOSSARY

armory—A storehouse for weapons.

artillery—The branch of the army specializing in the use of heavy mounted guns.

barracks—A group of buildings for lodging soldiers.

battalion—A military unit composed of a headquarters and two or more companies.

brigade—A military unit consisting of a variable number of men organized for a specific purpose.

casualties—Number of soldiers killed, wounded, captured, or missing.

cavalry—Troops trained to fight on horseback.

circuit—The act of riding around something.

Confederacy—The Southern states that seceded from the United States in 1860 and 1861.

courier—A messenger.

deploy—To station or place.

engage—To enter into conflict with.

epidemic—The sudden, rapid spread of an infectious disease.

esprit—Spirit; wit; liveliness.

flank—The right or left side of a military formation.

gallop—A fast three-beat gait of a horse in which all four feet are off the ground at the same time.

garrison—A permanently established military post.

harass—To trouble, worry, or torment.

infantry—Soldiers trained, armed, and equipped to fight on foot.

infatuated—Completely carried away by foolish or shallow love or affection.

inflated—Increased or raised beyond what is normal or valid.

militia—An army composed of citizens rather than professional soldiers.

outflank—To outmaneuver or outwit.

picket—A detachment of soldiers on guard duty.

plebe—A member of the freshman class at the United States Military Academy or Naval Academy.

precipice—A very steep cliff.

regiment—A military unit of ground troops consisting of at least two battalions.

renegade—A person who rejects one cause, or allegiance, for another.

rouse—To stir up, as to action.

saber—Sword.

screen—To prevent an army's movements from being detected.

secede—To formally withdraw from membership.

shank—The part of an instrument or a tool that connects the functioning part and the handle.

supply line—The route to provide food, materials, and equipment to an army.

trot—A moderately fast gait of a horse in which the legs move as diagonal pairs.

Union—The United States of America regarded as a national unit, especially during the Civil War.

Yankee—A Union soldier during the Civil War.

FURTHER READING

Boatner, Mark M. *The Civil War Dictionary*. New York: Vintage Books, 1991.

Civil War Society. *The American Civil War: A Multicultural Encyclopedia*. Danbury, Conn.: Grolier Education Corporation, 1994.

Davis, Burke. *Jeb Stuart: The Last Cavalier*. New York: Holt, Rinehart & Winston, 1957.

Hakim, Joy. *War, Terrible War*. New York: Oxford University Press, 1994.

Kent, Zachary. *The Civil War: "A House Divided."* Springfield, N.J.: Enslow Publishers, Inc., 1994.

Ketchum, Robert M. *American Heritage Picture History of the Civil War*. New York: American Heritage Publishing Co., 1960.

Robertson, James I., Jr. *Civil War: America Becomes One Nation*. New York: Alfred Knopf, 1992.

Thomas, Emory M. *Bold Dragoon: The Life of J.E.B. Stuart*. New York: Harper & Row, Publishers, 1986.

Ward, Geoffrey C. *The Civil War: An Illustrated History*. New York: Alfred A. Knopf, 1994.

INDEX